THE BIG IDEA

THE BIG IDEA

HOW TO MAKE YOUR ENTREPRENEURIAL
DREAMS COME TRUE, FROM THE
AHA MOMENT TO YOUR FIRST MILLION

Donny Deutsch

with Catherine Whitney

New York

To my girls,
Chelsey, London, and Daisy

Contents

Acknowledgments

've always said that if you want to be successful, surround yourself with people who are smarter than you. It's worked for me. Big ideas may start in the minds of individuals, but they flourish when passionate, creative, talented people come together. No individual is good at everything. Success is always a collaborative affair.

Writing this book is just another example. I didn't do it alone. Not even close. The idea to take the excitement of *The Big Idea* and translate it to book form was the vision of my good friend and literary agent, Wayne Kabak, a real pro; and a result of the astute sense of my Hyperion editor, Will Balliett, who saw the perfect formula—the special combination of inspiration and practical advice that makes this book unique in the field. They found a writer, Catherine Whitney, with the enthusiasm and skill to bring my philosophy, stories, and voice to life on the page. The result is something to be proud of, because it gives you a tactical blueprint while inspiring you to ask, "Why NOT me?"

I owe a special thanks to Stephanie Jones, my manager and director of communications, for all she does every day. Smart, positive, and ready to take on every challenge, Stephanie helped to make this book happen, even as she juggled many other roles. Huge Kudos to Lisa, Jenna, and Brittany, who brilliantly help me manage my days with wisdom, heart, and soul.

This book would not have been possible without the remarkable efforts of the team at CNBC. My show, *The Big Idea*, is the laboratory for the entrepreneurial spirit, and many of the inspiring stories in the book were first discovered through the show. I also have been blessed with a superior team of business experts, whose advice appears in the book.

Big shout out to Mark Hoffman, the dynamic leader of CNBC, whose support, vision, and patience have allowed *The Big Idea* to find its voice. He's also become a great friend. I owe much to my friend, the brilliant Susan Krakower, who launched the show and has always looked out for it and me as a fierce mother hen. I love her like a sister. Jonathan Wald has also always added guidance and smarts along with friendship; for that I am thankful. Thanks to Wilson Surratt for two great years executive producing *The Big Idea*. A huge thanks to Mary Duffy, a tireless, razor-sharp, wonderful human being and the day-to-day driver of *The Big Idea* ship, whom I'm eternally grateful to.

My colleagues at Deutsch Inc. remain my most reliable support system and the smartest team in advertising. Deutsch Inc. CEO Linda Sawyer continues to be a guiding force in my life. I'm deeply grateful to the community of entrepreneurs whose lives I've been privileged to share. I'm the luckiest guy in the world, because every day I get to go to work and be amazed, inspired, and motivated. It's my greatest pleasure to share that excitement with you.

Finally, to Dad and Mom, who always encouraged me to follow my dreams, who picked me up when I stumbled, and who have showed by their example what it means to live a life of dignity and possibility in a crazy world.

What's The Big Idea?

CHAPTER 1

Calling
All Dreamers

- A carpenter gets tired of almost losing a finger whenever he slices a bagel. Bam! Bagel Guillotine.
- A homemaker is frustrated that her pantry is full of stale food because the packages don't stay closed. Bam! Quick Seals.
- A woman is annoyed that her bra strap keeps slipping. Bam! Strap Tamers.
- A nutrition-conscious couple wants frozen foods that aren't junk. Bam! Amy's Kitchen.
- A mother is worn out from chasing down runny-nosed kids. Bam! Boogie Wipes.
- A stylish lady is fed up with visible panty lines. Bam! Spanx.

Big ideas are all around us. Every day I meet people who have come up with innovations that nobody ever thought of before. In each case, the idea grew out of a need, something that was missing, a frustration, the desire to make life a little easier, a little better. These are slap-yourself-on-the-side-of-the head, obvious ideas. But it took people with the desire and motivation to see them through.

If *you're* sitting on a big idea right now—an idea that could make you millions—it's time to get moving. Don't let anything stop you. Don't let anyone dismiss your idea and tell you that your dream won't work. When in doubt, *do*.

The American dream is within your reach. I've literally seen it happen hundreds of times. The people who turn their big ideas into millions come from every conceivable background. They're middle-class moms, factory workers, college kids, veterans, people with disabilities, office workers, retirees, everyone and anyone. Ordinary people—some faced with enormous obstacles—are stepping up and achieving extraordinary goals.

They share one thing in common. They were passionate about their ideas—so passionate that when the naysayers piled on, they kept shrugging them off, believing they could achieve their desires . . . and they did. They acted on their beliefs. And their achievements represent a revolution that's sweeping across our nation, changing the way business is done.

News flash: We no longer live in a top-down world. We live in an age of individual empowerment. The business culture has undergone the most radical transformation since the Industrial Revolution. Turning individual dreams into reality is much more possible than ever before. The smart ones are those who figure out how to get a piece of the action.

Forget the old excuses. Drop the *Us* vs. *Them* mentality. You don't need a corporation to make it. You don't need your own factory to produce a product. You don't even need an office. From your home, you can build your own Web site, do your own research, create an electronic sales force, join a community of like-minded people, and sell your product.

Dreaming is the new reality, and *The Big Idea* is the ultimate reality show. My guests are the embodiment of everything that's wonderful and hopeful about who we are as a culture in the twenty-first century. They didn't make it because they were born into the lucky sperm club, or were the best-looking folks in the room, or even were especially talented. These are people who through human drive and passion—and yeah, sometimes a little luck—found their way to the mountaintop.

There are many different roads to success. But I have to say, on a personal level, there's nothing I enjoy more than coming across someone who was a screwup as a kid and is now making it.

Who Am I to Talk?

Why do I relate to former screwups so well? Because I speak from experience—I was once that kid. I want you to know a little about me, so you'll understand where I'm coming from. The rap on me was always: "Donny's got the brains—if only he'd apply himself."

My parents and teachers knew I was smart, and it frustrated the hell out of them that I seemed unable to buckle down. Frankly, school bored me. Getting good grades wasn't important to me. Having fun was. I was a strategic genius on the playground, but when the bell rang and I was placed in a classroom, I was adrift. I was full of energy—restless, distracted, a big talker, but lousy on the follow-through. The phrase I kept hearing repeated was: "Donny! Pay attention." The problem was clear to me even then: I had the attention span of a gnat. Today they probably would have diagnosed me with ADD and medicated the restlessness right out of me. Maybe it would have been for the better, but I'm glad they didn't. With the benefit of a lot of hindsight, I *own* that kid. That was the real me.

Every successful person has an element of luck in their lives, and my parents were my lucky card. I grew up in Hollis Hills, Queens, and had a nice upper-middle-class life. My parents encouraged me every day, even when I gave them plenty of reasons to tear their hair out. Sometimes they used the carrot, and sometimes they used the stick, but they never gave up on me. They always saw my potential.

My dad worked in advertising. He was a creative director at the big agency Ogilvy & Mather, before deciding to open up his own shop, David Deutsch Associates. He always advised me, "Do what you love," which was a pretty radical concept back then. Generally, though, the message was that fun was for the weekends. Work was serious business. The mountaintop in my youth was being a professional man—a doctor, a lawyer, an accountant.

There was no place for dreamers in the classroom. The future was mapped out—study hard, get into a decent college, land a good job, settle down. That was the success model in those days. People didn't talk about finding yourself. The playbook for happiness was based on fitting into one of the standard boxes. If I have any advice for parents today—and now that I am a parent, I include myself—it's to pay attention to what your kid loves and nurture it.

School was a grind for me, but there were glimmers of hope, moments when I shined. If I'd understood myself better, I would have jumped on them, seen the area of my potential. I could talk my way out of any scrape and I was even elected class president my senior year in high school. What I lacked in discipline, I tried to make up for in charm, and sometimes it worked. I had a six brain and a ten mouth.

I never saw the obvious—that I could translate my people skills into a career path. As I approached the end of my high school years, the sole focus was on getting my grades up and passing the tests so I could get into a good college. My first hint that maybe I did have an intellect after all was when I did well on the Regents tests. It's a funny thing about standardized tests. Sometimes kids with totally mediocre grades ace them, to everyone's amazement. In the essay portion of the Regents, I demonstrated to myself that I could think and write creatively. It was a revelation to me.

I knuckled down enough to get into the University of Pennsylvania, but I was still restless and eager to get on with my life in the real world. When I graduated from Wharton, I went to work for Ogilvy & Mather, the corporate giant of advertising. I had the typical mentality of a new graduate: Go with the best. I thought this would be my proving ground.

Was I ever wrong. On *so* many counts! For one thing, since I was a business school graduate, I got slotted on the account side and ended up being the worst account executive in the history of advertising. At Ogilvy & Mather I was assigned to the Maxwell House coffee account at a very, very junior level. There was a scary kind of passion in that place that wasn't at all positive. My first day on the job, I walked into a meeting and the tension was so thick I couldn't breathe. I didn't get it. Those people looked like they were going to blow a gasket. It wasn't an energizing, creative kind of mood. It was a desperate, terrified energy. They were definitely not having fun. I wanted to shout into the crowded room, "Hey, lighten up. It's only coffee." *Only* coffee! Shows what a pinhead I was.

As an assistant account executive, I was really just a glorified numbers cruncher. I wanted to get out and meet the clients. But I was told that no one at my level ever met clients. So I sat in my miserable cubicle and hated every minute of it. The culture of Ogilvy & Mather at the time was antithetical to my nature. This is why it's so important to know yourself. Some people thrive in big corporate cultures. I wasn't one of them. It took me about nine months to figure out that it was a bad fit. They should have fired me; I quit before they could.

But I wasn't done establishing myself as a screwup. Seeing that I was drifting, my dad made an extremely generous offer. He invited me to join his agency, and I accepted.

My dad had created a solid, conservative boutique agency with a reputation for classy print advertising. I wanted to get involved in the creative work, maybe shake things up, but Dad put me in my place. "You're a business grad. We need you on the account side." At least I got to meet clients this time, but my heart wasn't in it. I'm sure the others in the agency whispered about what a jerk the boss's son was.

Dad saw things clearly, and he gave me some tough love: "Get the hell out of here. Find something you're passionate about."

Now, being fired by my father hurt. I was twenty-six years old, had bailed on my first two jobs, and it felt like the end of the world. I was embarrassed and depressed. One thing seemed glaringly obvious: I was not cut out for the world of advertising. I needed to go in a completely different direction. So, I decided to become a lawyer!

I hit the books, took the law school tests, and had just been accepted at George Washington University Law School when something happened that changed my life forever.

My dad told me he was going to sell the agency. He was in his mid-fifties, and he'd had a good offer from a Philadelphia group. His plan was to sell David Deutsch Assoc., work there a few more years, and then retire. He had it all mapped out. And when he told me about it, something inside me screamed, "Wait a minute!"

That was my wake-up call. For the first time in my life, I listened to my gut, and my gut told me to challenge the decision. It felt wrong. Deep down, I didn't think my dad really wanted to sell. And I had a vision. I went to him and poured my heart out. I asked him not to sell. I asked him to bring me back, not on the account side, but as a creative engine to generate new business and new ideas. I was convinced I could build the agency. It was the most impassioned speech I had ever given.

It says a lot about my dad that he listened to me, and didn't start ticking off all my false starts and screwups. I was asking him to give up a lot of money and take a chance on me. And he said yes! I'm still amazed that he agreed. I can only imagine how many sleepless nights he had over that decision. But his faith in me changed my life.

In 1983, the agency had thirty employees. Over the next eighteen years, I helped turn Deutsch into a major contender in the ad world. I was on fire. No account was too big for us to pitch. By 2000, we had one thousand employees and a slate of big-name clients like Ikea, Pfizer, Mitsubishi, Revlon, and Bank of America. I like to say I was a late starter and a strong finisher. But what actually happened to turn me around?

When my dad agreed to give me the freedom to develop his agency, it was my moment of truth: *Put up or shut up.* Two factors drove me forward. The first was laying it all on the line, not just for myself, but for my dad. I couldn't let either of us down. The second was that finally, at the ripe old age of twenty-six, I had found my passion. I was in love with my work.

Love Is the Answer

If I've asked two thousand people, "What's the secret to your success?" almost every answer is identical: "Do what you love." You have to be passionate about it. I'll take it a step further: No matter what you do, if you're not passionate about it, find something else.

I have never met a truly successful person who was not fired up about their work. Take a look at the icons in business today—the Donald Trumps, the Rupert Murdochs—and you'll see the gleam in their eyes. These guys have so much money, they don't have to work another minute of their lives. They work because it turns them on. You want to know who's doing well? Notice the people with the big shit-eating grins on their faces.

There are a lot of ways to measure success. Money is one way. But the key is love. Most of our waking hours are spent working, and if you don't love what you're doing, you're not going to be happy day-to-day.

Here's a clue: When Sunday night feels as great as Friday night, you're doing what you love. I still remember when I worked at Ogilvy & Mather, Friday night was the peak of my week. My real life, my happiness, my pleasure all happened on the weekend. By Sunday night I was winding down, feeling tense, gearing up for a five-day grind.

To this day I can recall how dramatically that changed once I really got engaged in my dad's agency. Sunday nights were as good as Friday nights. No, they were *better*. I couldn't wait to get to work. My work was my play. It was fun for me. And that's when I started getting successful. So, if Sunday night is your Friday night, you're in the right place.

Our business tradition in this country is pretty stoic. As a society we still have trouble with the idea that happiness is consistent with success. That "no pain, no gain" philosophy has stuck to us like glue. The rubric is to work hard for forty years, then retire and enjoy yourself. What a messed-up plan! There are plenty of retirees on golf courses asking themselves, "Is that all there is?"

When people get it that work can be fun, it's a huge revelation. I see a lot of transformation on my show. I hear the wildest stories. Only they're not so wild when you see the results. I had a guy, Nathan Sawaya, a big corporate lawyer earning in the high six figures. One day he chucked it all to become a thirteen-dollar-an-hour LEGOs builder at LEGOLAND. It turns out that from the time he was four he loved LEGOs. I mean, *passionately* loved them. In college, he had LEGOs under the bed in his dorm. So, now he decided to go back to his first love. You can imagine what his family and friends thought of that idea! Think of the conversation: "Honey, I'm going to leave my corporate job and build LEGOs for a living." But here's the punch line. Today Nathan is one of the premiere LEGO artists in the world. He earns thousands of dollars for his original works of art. And why not?

Nathan's creations convey emotion, subtlety, and humor—all through this unexpected medium that most people would consider child's play. He's a happy guy.

Nathan hit on a very important secret to success. When people ask me how to go about finding their passion, I use Nathan as an example. Go back to your childhood, which was the purest time in your life. What did you love? What were your hobbies? We tend to divide our lives into work and play. Look at the play. I guarantee you'll find an insight into what makes you happy today.

In fact, that's how I got into television, *The Big Idea* . . . and now this book!

In 2000, I sold our agency to an international holding company, Interpublic, for around three hundred million dollars. I was still the CEO, but I was less involved. By this point in my life, I knew myself pretty well, and I saw that the agency was no longer capturing my heart and soul as completely as it once had. I'd been doing this for too long. I'd walk into a meeting and figure out in the first five seconds what was going to happen. I loved the business, but the sense of great challenges was no longer there for me. I was feeling restless, not engaged one hundred percent. I knew what that meant. As is my nature, I started scouting around, looking for a new mountain to climb. I found it at CNBC.

Of course, it didn't happen overnight. CNBC had always called on me over the years for commentary and opinions on marketing-related topics for their business shows. Whenever they wanted "the ad guy" they came to me, and I always enjoyed it. My agency was featured on Donald Trump's *The Apprentice*, and that got a lot of attention. After I substituted as a host on *Kudlow & Cramer*, I said to myself, "Why not pitch an idea for a show?"

I'd noticed that every time I did TV I got a rush. I was pumped. The folks at CNBC noticed it, too. It didn't matter that I had no real experience in television. This time I had enough business experience under my belt that I was confident I could add value.

I thought, "Why NOT me?" When I have met the most successful people, almost without exception they have that "Why NOT me?" sense of entitlement. You could line up thousands of other people with the same skills, but they have that extra bit of "Screw it, I should be doing it." And that was my attitude.

It wasn't easy, and it was a big emotional risk. Obviously, by that point I wasn't going to the poorhouse if it didn't work, but there was no guarantee that I could make it in TV. In fact, history proved that the odds would be against me. Only a small percentage of new talk shows make it. The first couple of years were tough. We had the name, *The Big Idea*, but we weren't paying homage to it. It was basically an interview show, and, to be honest, I found it a little boring. We kept experimenting, and CNBC, led by its dynamic president, Mark Hoffman, gave us support, patience, and room to grow and change. And we finally found our big idea in the lives of remarkable people—not just celebrities, but ordinary folks who transformed themselves with guts and passion. Within a year we went from one night a week to five nights. Over time, we got the right formula, and today *The Big Idea* has become a real winner.

Once again, I had found an arena where my ten-mouth was a plus. And once again, I love my work. A friend recently tagged the show "Inspirational entertainment." He hit the nail on the head. And I think I'm the guy who is most inspired by the people who come on my show. I really feel like a kid in a candy store.

How do you find what you love? It's got to start at the gut level.

Listen to the Little Voice

Trusting your gut is a win-win situation. You might think, "What does my gut know?" A lot. That nagging little voice inside is telling you what you truly know, think, and believe.

Hey, you could be wrong, but it's real. It's you. Listen to it. Take advantage of it.

You already know this is true in life. You probably trust your gut a hundred times a day and don't even realize it. From the moment you roll out of bed and start preparing for the day, you're bombarded by choices. Some just feel right. You wouldn't be able to dress yourself if you didn't trust your gut. And of course, we put a lot of store in the concept of chemistry when choosing a mate or a business partner. What is chemistry but a deep response from the gut?

This same gut-sense is important in business, too. Yet so many people ignore the inner voice and end up trudging through their professional lives feeling unfulfilled. Instead of tuning in to their hearts, they follow the cacophony of the chorus about what they're supposed to be doing, or what is most prestigious, or what is the safest path. Well, I have news for you. Prestigious jobs can be boring and soul-deadening. And the safest, most conventional route doesn't guarantee success, much less joy.

I had a great woman on the show named Taryn Rose. She is a gutsy lady who listened to her heart and won. Taryn was a self-described "good Vietnamese girl" who always did what her parents wanted. And what they wanted most was for their daughter to become a doctor, so she obediently went to medical school and became an orthopedic surgeon. She was a good one, too. The only problem was that she hated it. "It seemed like death," she told me. "I could see myself for the rest of my life doing the same ten procedures." She took a good look at her life and asked the critical question, "If I don't love what I'm doing now, when do I think I will?"

Taryn's head and a lifetime of conditioning was telling her one thing. Her gut was telling her another. If she listened to her gut, she'd be going against everything she'd ever been taught.

So she took a big leap because she didn't want to be sixty and say, "I wish I'd done that."

Taryn's big idea grew organically out of her practice. Her patients had foot pain, and that meant having to wear those ugly orthopedic shoes that made them feel old and unsexy. She often heard from patients that they'd rather suffer than look like their grandmothers. It bothered her that there wasn't a hot, luxury shoe that was both comfortable and sexy. So she invented one.

Going from being an orthopedic surgeon to a shoe designer was a pretty big leap of faith, and it was definitely not a "good girl" move. Her parents didn't speak to her for a year. There were many dark moments. But today Taryn Rose shoes are sold in every high-end department store internationally, and Taryn has five locations.

How did she know to trust her gut on such a major life change? Here's Taryn's litmus test: "If you can imagine yourself in the future looking back and feeling sad that you didn't go for it, that's how you know."

By nature, anything new comes from the soul. The day you stop listening to your inner voice, the dream dies.

An Act of Life

On *The Big Idea*, we celebrate people who have the courage and stamina to make their dreams come true. But in every case, the road to success starts with an idea.

Some people think a big idea is like a lightning bolt out of the blue that slams you in the head. You know, that "Aha!" thing. But it's hardly ever like that. The big idea isn't an act of God. It's an act of daily life. Simply put, the idea that will make millions starts with an observation. It comes down to a keen awareness of your life and the lives around you. It's the moment when you say, "There's gotta be a better way." It's the moment when you ask, "How can I solve this problem?" It's the moment when you see something and think, "Huh, maybe that will work in my neigh-borhood." The real big ideas are organic. They come from life.

Look around. What are the most successful companies today—the big ideas people really admire? How did they get started? With an observation. Starbucks originated after Howard Schultz noticed on a trip to Italy that there were coffee bars on almost every corner. He loved the quality of the brew, but what really caught his attention was the feeling of a public living room. He asked the question: "Why couldn't that work at home?"

Federal Express was started by a regular guy named Fred Smith who saw the potential for an overnight delivery service. He wrote a college term paper about how it could transform the business world. "I probably got my usual C on that paper," he said. But today FedEx is a twenty-seven-billion-dollar company.

Whole Foods originated as a health food store in John Mack-ey's garage in Austin, Texas. He saw a need for fresh, healthy foods that wasn't being met. Today it's the largest retailer of natural and organic foods in the country.

In each case, a need was not being met. A problem had to be solved. And these innovators stepped up to the plate and took action. None of them had a barrel of cash. None of them had a ton of experience. They started with a moment of awareness and followed it through.

Awareness is the ignition. Motivation is the accelerator. That's when you say, "Where am I going to go with it? What ac-tion am I going to take?" No action, no story.

Most people who don't get their ideas into being are stuck at the point of motivation. It's easy to say, "I have an idea." Every-body's got an idea. But you have to do something to put faith into action.

Usually it's a matter of taking baby steps. It could mean walk-ing into a store and looking around. Or going to a trade show. Or drawing a picture of your idea. Or asking five friends to try it.

Every action moves you one notch further. The impediments are fear and negativity:

"I don't know how . . ."

"It's not that good . . ."

"I've never made anything before . . ."

"I'm too busy . . ."

"I don't have the money . . ."

"If it was such a good idea, someone else would have done it . . ."

And on and on. There are endless reasons *not* to do it. Anyone can whip themselves into a frenzy of fear. That's easier than rolling over and going to sleep. It's those who respond to the wake-up call that make it.

What's inspirational about our show is that viewers see people they can identify with who put one foot in front of another, and didn't let their inner voice of doubt win. These are people who believed in themselves and forged ahead, even when one hundred people said no. I like the way one of my guests put it: "When someone says *no*, I don't hear *no*. I hear *not that way*."

My Promise to You

Okay, let's cut to the chase. I've told you something about who I am and what I believe. Here's what I have to offer.

The Big Idea is hitting a nerve. Viewers take our motto to heart—we call the show "your daily road map to the American dream"—and they tune in every night to bring that jolt of possibility into their living rooms. We get hundreds of e-mails, calls, and letters after every show. Across the board, people are asking for two things: inspiration and utility. There are plenty of books out there that have motivational messages, and plenty more that offer practical tools. *The Big Idea* brings a special formula to the table, and I'm going to share it with you. In this book I'll bring to life the true, inspirational stories of regular people who got started with little more than a dream and an idea, and take you through the process of how they overcame barriers and made it work.

On the show, we create a mutually beneficial arena. I am endlessly fascinated by the question—which I ask every guest— *"How did you do it?"* I want to know the minute details. What were the steps? What happened, and then what happened, and then what happened? In return, I give them the best advice I have on everything from getting the first sale to finding an investor to picking a name to making a profit. The synergy is electric.

When you finish reading this book, I promise you, you'll have two things: You'll be charged up, and you'll have a knowledge base. The next step is up to you.

Are you ready to get off the bench?

Great! Let's make it happen!

CHAPTER 2

No Experience
Necessary

W hen *The Big Idea* first went on the air, everyone wanted me to take lessons. They suggested hiring a TV coach, a seasoned pro, to show me how to do it. I was new to television, and they couldn't wait to whip me into shape—to infuse me with that familiar TV style. But if I was the brand they were buying, I had to be myself.

Of course, I don't resist everything about television. I have the makeup people around before I go on air, to powder my nose and futz with my hair. And I have a truly great team in every capacity. The point I'm making here is more profound. People are looking for authenticity—the real deal. And sometimes having no experience—for me, going on TV without extensive training and coaching—can give you an edge.

So many people come on my show and say, "The reason I was so successful is that I didn't know what I didn't know." Their point is they didn't know they couldn't succeed, so they just jumped in. This is the ultimate example of turning a deterrent into a motivator. If you aren't aware of the enormous boulders that lie strewn in your path, you're more likely to go for it. Then, when you hit the boulders, you'll find ways of navigating around them.

One of the reasons I was so successful building the Deutsch agency is that I didn't come up through a traditional agency system. I didn't know I wasn't supposed to do some of the things I tried. I was naïve enough to think a crazy idea could work, and it did. Organizationally, I built an agency that was different from the way an agency was supposed to be.

It was really tough getting my own show up and running, but being inexperienced, I wasn't gun-shy. This is a constant theme of successful upstarts.

Ignorance can become your bliss. It worked for me.

What You Don't Know Won't Hurt You

Inexperience enables you to get on the path and move. Sometimes when people talk about "the voice of experience," they're referring to a guy who is so beaten down, he's paralyzed. If you don't believe me, just think about political officials. A politician gets elected for the first time, and everyone is all jazzed about a fresh face, a bold new voice. Four years down the road, that fresh face is looking a little tight. The voice has turned cautious. Maybe it's human nature. But don't be so scared of being the new kid on the block. You can use it to your advantage.

For example, I always say that the person who is going to develop the next great drink will not necessarily be from the drink industry. The old pros have too many obstacles in their heads: *Oh, that packaging could never work. Oh, shelf space is too hard to get. Do you realize how impossible it is to get into Pathmark?*

The naïve newcomer may fall flat on his or her face, but sometimes a lack of experience is what makes the idea fly. Lizzy Morrill came up against this when she tried to launch Fizzy Lizzy, a sparkling juice drink. People said, "If it's such a good idea, why hasn't Coke or Pepsi come up with it?" That's the kind of challenge that will stop you dead in your tracks. Lizzy didn't let it. She had something of the rebel spirit in her. "When an expert said no, it made me even more determined."

Like most great ideas, Lizzy's moment of clarity came from a practical problem. She loved mixing fruit juice with seltzer. One day she was riding her bike across Long Island's North Shore, awkwardly juggling bottles of juice and seltzer. She had a thought bubble: "Wouldn't it be great if I could have this all in one bottle?" There were some products out there, but they were loaded with sweeteners or other unnatural ingredients. She was going for an all-natural mix.

She got to work in her tiny kitchen mixing batches until she found the taste she liked. The anecdotal feedback from friends gave her the impetus to take it to the next step. In all Lizzy made over one hundred phone calls before she found a bottler. If you're afraid of hearing no, let Lizzy be your inspiration. Along with the rejection, everyone she called gave her the same piece of damning advice: "The odds are against you." She didn't quit. Finally, a food scientist became a partner (she gave him two percent of the business), and she was able to get a batch made. From there it was all legwork and lots of heavy lifting, lugging her glass bottles around Manhattan. In seven years, she broke into one specialty store after another and got her product on the shelves. Looking back, Lizzy has no

Big Idea Lesson: Lizzy is a model of tenacity, but she also made some smart decisions along the way. One of these was the decision to give up a small percentage of her business to partner with an expert who could make it happen. She saw that 98 percent of *something* was better than 100 percent of *nothing*.

regrets about her long struggle to make it. I enjoy Lizzy's spirit. As she told me, "I didn't have a boyfriend. I didn't have a baby. I thought I could have a juice."

If she'd known all the barriers that were on the road to getting her product produced and in stores, would Lizzy have chucked it from the start? Maybe, maybe not. The point is that her arena of possibility was much greater because she didn't know about the hurdles. She took them as they came and kept going.

Everybody Loves an Underdog

The next time you get anxious about being the little guy, remember this truth of business and life: Everybody loves an underdog. Think about it. Do you root for David or do you root for Goliath? In my early days at Deutsch, when we were small and feisty, we had a tremendous emotional advantage. I loved going into client presentations and having people look at me like, "Who does this guy think he is?" I knew we had the goods, and I got a charge out of going up against the big guys. One of our first major pitches, when we were still a pretty tiny agency, was for the Ikea account. All the first-tier agencies were pitching, and the word on the street was that Chiat/Day, a real heavy hitter, was the favorite. We went in there and blew away the competition. Why? The client loved our work and loved our edginess. But on an emotional level, I'm convinced that the people in the room were attracted to our underdog status and our raw hunger. They knew we'd give our all—and we did.

It may feel a little counterintuitive. Many new businesses are obsessed with demonstrating that they're bigger and more established than they are. They seek credibility by giving the impression of experience. But sometimes the advantage is with the business that is struggling to get a foothold and manifests hunger. Recognize when that's true and run with it.

Remember this: People *want to* help you when you're just starting out. When Lindsay Wieber and Gwen Whiting had the idea of luxury laundry goods, they had zero experience and even less cash to get their business off the ground. To launch The Laundress they held a fund-raiser—a "for profit" party—and in-

Big Idea Lesson: **When you tap into that human desire to help—when you ask people to give you a chance, give you a leg up, cheer you on—the result can be a miraculous outpouring of support.**

vited everyone they knew. The cover charge was fifteen dollars. Their friends and family loved the idea. They raised five thousand dollars from the party, and their business was launched. Every person who came to the party felt good about it.

Fake It Till You Make It

I get a kick out of the college kids who come on the show—the ones who got their million-dollar ideas under way while they were still in school. I admire them. I was pretty tuned out during my college years. The last thing that would have occurred to me was to get off my butt and start a business.

Two University of Florida kids went from the frat house to a franchise worth over fifty million dollars. Matt Friedman and Adam Scott wanted buffalo wings, and there were none to be found in Gainesville—at least, none that met their standards. So they cooked up a recipe in the frat house kitchen, word got out, and soon they were filling orders on a daily basis, taking in around five hundred dollars a night—not chump change for a college kid.

Finally, the university caught on and told them they couldn't use the frat house kitchen anymore. So they put on their best suits and starting hitting the banks. They had a lot of chutzpah and a strong pitch, but the loan officers were underwhelmed. (I'd like to meet those loan officers today, and ask them if they're

Big Idea Lesson: If you have a big idea, money is never an object. To fund their enterprise, these young entrepreneurs did what investors often advise—they went to family first.

kicking themselves.) Finally, they did what I often advise people to do as a first step—they went to their parents. Each set of parents loaned them five thousand dollars on two conditions— that they consider it a loan, not a gift, and that they stay in school. The first outpost of The Wing Zone was run on a shoe-string and a prayer. Today they have a hundred franchises across the country.

From Battlefield to Boardroom

We can all learn a big lesson from the retired military veterans who have become successful entrepreneurs. No one deserves a share of the American dream more than these guys. They may not have practical business experience, but they have something more valuable—real life experience.

Glen Meakem, a retired captain who served in the first Gulf War and is now a multimillionaire venture capitalist, told us on *The Big Idea*, "I owe my success to what I learned in the military." The experience gained from leading troops in a war zone provided Glen with an amazing training ground for business.

Those lessons included: the need for extraordinary team-work, the discipline to see a mission through from start to finish, and the daily gut check that required him to learn to manage and control his fears. When Glen returned to the United States, he put those lessons to use, creating FreeMarkets, a precursor to eBay that provided a revolutionary system of corporate purchasing. He later sold the company for five hundred million dollars. The risk of starting a new company in an unfamiliar city—Pittsburgh—

did not daunt Glen. What was the worst thing that could happen? He'd already seen the worst, on the battlefield.

Teamwork, discipline, and courage are winning combinations in both life and work. The former soldiers I interview all have them. Experience in the military can make up for inexperience in the marketplace.

Big Idea Lesson: The inner resources built through discipline, training, and raw life experience can be a solid foundation for business success.

Your Lucky Napkin

Amilya Antonetti has become one of the mainstays of *The Big Idea*'s panel of experts, and if you watch the show you've seen her in action. Amilya embodies the heart and soul of what we're all about—a compelling personal story, a great idea that serves a real need, the drive to break into a daunting market, and a major success. She also radiates a boundless energy and a determined optimism that are pretty compelling and charming, all at the same time.

Amilya's company Soapworks all started with a moment of clarity in the midst of a life-and-death battle.

When Amilya's son David was an infant, she was constantly taking him to the emergency room. He suffered repeated bouts of terrible breathing difficulties, severe rashes, and unexplained tantrums. Something was very wrong, but no doctor could explain his symptoms. On more than one occasion, David was at death's door. The medical experts could not help, so Amilya knew it was up to her to save her son. She began an excavation of their lives, looking for clues, and discovered that soon after she cleaned their home each Tuesday, David's symptoms took a turn for the worse. Her son was suffering severe allergic reactions to common home cleaning products. Unfortunately, when she went looking for hypoallergenic cleaning products, there were none to be found. Her grandmother suggested she make her own soap, using a recipe she'd once used herself. Amilya began mixing batches in her kitchen. Soon David's health was improving, and her family and friends began clamoring for the product. She became the neighborhood soap lady. That's when Amilya realized that she had a real service to provide. People needed her soap!

In 1994, Amilya began shopping her soap to supermarket chains, and she ran smack into a brick wall. The response was derisive. They'd say, "Honey, have you ever heard of Clorox? Have you ever heard of Tide?" Repeatedly, buyers told Amilya that their customers would not be interested in hypoallergenic products. She knew that they were wrong. On one occasion, she marched back into a buyer's office and declared, "*I* am your customer."

Amilya was convinced that a population of people just like herself wasn't being served. She kept pushing, conducting her own market research among customers in grocery store aisles. She used every dollar she had—she sold her car, closed out savings accounts, turned in CDs—whatever it was going to take to make her soaps a reality and to compete with some of the largest corporations in the world.

More than a decade later, Amilya's Soapworks is a sixty-million-dollar business that has pioneered a new way of cleaning that is healthy and natural, while educating the public about the harmful effects of the chemicals in ordinary household products. Amilya accomplished this with a never-say-die attitude and good, old-fashioned legwork. Today, her products can be found on the shelves of national grocery chain and specialty stores.

Amilya is obviously just the kind of success story we love to feature on *The Big Idea*. But there's more. Something happened during Amilya's first appearance that changed her life again. Toward the end of the show, I asked Amilya, "So, what's next?" She hadn't expected the question, but in a few seconds she poured out her life's passion for helping others find their dreams and get their ideas birthed from "mind to market." She didn't think much of it at the time, so Amilya was astonished when five thousand viewers responded with ideas and questions. With that inspiration, she knew she had to find a way to bring all the tools, tips, and resources together. She wanted to be able to help more people be heard, as well as help them give birth to their ideas.

As Amilya reflected on her own journey and the difficulties she faced getting her product to market, she realized how much easier it would have been if she'd had a community to support and advise her. So she decided to create one. Lucky Napkin is a venture launched by Amilya and three like-minded, successful entrepreneurs, to help launch and grow big ideas. This is a great resource for anyone who is ready to take an idea from the back of a napkin to the heart of the market.

BIG IDEA TOOLBOX
BEGINNER'S ROAD MAP

Our *Big Idea* experts are ready to help you get off the ground. Check out their Web sites for a treasure trove of practical advice you can start using today.

* Lucky Napkin (www.luckynapkin.com): Amilya Antonetti and her team of experts help people launch their business ideas.
* Edge Consulting (www.drdoug.com): Dr. Doug Hirschhorn,

(continued)

a leading performance coach, shows you how to get the job done.

* Obsidian Launch (www.obsidianlaunch.com): Michael Michalowicz partners with first-time entrepreneurs who are willing to give their all.

* Smallbiztechnology (www.smallbiztechnology.com): Ramon Ray shows how to use technology to grow a business.

You can also go to *The Big Idea* Web site (www.cnbc.com) to complement the guidance you'll receive in this book.

The World Is Your Classroom

Now, here's the caveat. When I say that there can be an inherent benefit in lack of experience, that doesn't mean you should be a jerk. Inexperience plus arrogance equals failure. Inexperience plus ignorance also equals failure. The most successful entrepreneurs are hungry to learn. They are obsessed with getting all the information they can about the industry, the market, and the competition. But this learning process does not happen in the abstract. Your classroom is the street. Here are some tips for getting quickly up to speed.

+ *Without realizing it, you may already have a core of advisers. Think about family members, friends, and colleagues and where they excel. Does your former college roommate raise money for charity? Pick her brain about the ins and outs of capital development. Is your brother an ad sales rep? Find out what he knows about reaching a niche market. Does your mother organize bake sales for your church?*

NO EXPERIENCE NECESSARY **29**

*She may have a wealth of knowledge about enlisting coop-
eration, event planning, and display. Has your father been
attending an industry trade show for his company for the
past twenty years? Find out everything you can about the
ins and outs of trade shows.*

+ *Dedicate at least one hour a day—religiously—to learning
about starting a business. Go online, visit a bookstore, park
yourself at the library, and gather as much information as
you can.*

+ *Join a local business group. Most communities have organizations such as the Chamber of Commerce and Women
in Business that host lunches and seminars. Even if your
business is not off the ground, you'll be welcome. These are
great places to learn and network.*

+ *Keep a notebook with you at all times. You never know
when you're going to learn something invaluable.*

DONNY'S DO: YOUR SMART TEAM

Be sure to hook up with people who know more than you do. Get your Smart Team behind you as a backup. I have always made it a policy to surround myself with people who are smarter than me. I was the catalyst, the vision person, and I always believed I was the key to the engine. But an engine has a lot of parts.

Don't hesitate to give your team opportunities to show you what they can do, what they can bring to the table to support your vision. You know you can't do it alone, so you assemble your team, and then let them go to it by assigning specific tasks. No one is good at everything. For example, I am terrible at organizing and keeping track of details. The most valuable people on my staff are those with a gift for keeping a hundred balls in the air at once. I couldn't do it without them.

CHAPTER **3**

Why Make Someone Else Rich?

E very day, whether I'm at Deutsch or at CNBC, I walk past hundreds of cubicles. I know for a fact that most of the people sitting in them have dreams that extend far beyond the few square feet of real estate they inhabit. If I stopped and asked each person, "What would you really love to be doing?" I'm sure that only a small percentage would say, "I'm doing it right now." Within every worker is a vision.

There's no question that younger workers today are less inclined than previous generations to settle for less. The American dream used to be about making someone else rich, and if you could grab a tiny piece of that pie, good for you. Today's kids—that's the last thing they want. They want the whole pie and the dish it came in. They have a sense of entitlement. Some people think that's a bad thing. I hate it when I hear the old geezers complaining because kids today don't want to suffer like they did. I think it's fuckin' great. I applaud that can-do spirit—but how do you make it happen? How do you rise above your cubicle?

The first thing you have to know is that it's up to you. No one else is going to do it for you. I remember when I was growing up, there were all these stories about big stars that were "discovered" walking down the street or sitting at the counter of a drugstore (drugstores had soda fountains in those days). And I used to think, wouldn't it be fantastic to have someone tap me on the shoulder and say, "Kid, I'm gonna make you rich"? Well, that's a one in a million kind of deal. But you wouldn't believe how many people are sitting around today just waiting for someone to tap them on the shoulder. The world isn't built that way.

Sometimes people get lucky, but even luck isn't purely arbitrary. Luck is attracted to passion. If you want the gods to smile on you, wear a smile. Have some passion, a sparkle in your eye. Passion is infectious.

I can't tell you how many times people have said to me, "I don't have the options of some of the people on your show. I have a family to feed. I can't just chuck my job to follow my dream." I tell them that nothing's easy. But everything is possible. You just have to take those baby steps.

One day I was talking to Meredith Applebaum, a talent producer for *The Big Idea*. She was telling me of her dream to someday start an image consulting business. I could tell she was passionate about it. Her whole face lit up when she talked about her love for fashion and style, and her natural eye for what worked.

"So, why don't you do it?" I asked.

Meredith looked at me as if I had three heads. "I can't . . . I have a job," she said. "I have bills to pay." Duh!

"Never say I can't," I told her. "You want to know how you can do it? I'll tell you. This Saturday, you're going to get your first client. You're going to find a guy you know and you're going to take him shopping. You're going to give him a wardrobe makeover. Then, next Saturday you're going to take another friend. Do this for ten weeks and you'll have a client base and a portfolio. On the eleventh week, charge five hundred dollars. These are baby steps, and it requires you to work weekends. But that's how businesses get built."

Well, Meredith took my advice. Not only that, it worked. A year later, she was handing in her resignation to start her own company. We were sorry to see Meredith go, but everyone on the show was inspired as well. Our farewell gift was to give her a segment on the show.

Could it really be that simple? If you have that all-important sense of entitlement, a fire in the belly, and the courage to follow your dreams—yes, it's just that simple.

The Soul of an Entrepreneur

I first met Jen Groover when she came on *The Big Idea* to pitch her innovative handbag, the Butler Bag. This is a great product that solves a big problem. Jen created it out of her own frustration with never being able to find stuff in her purse. She was tired of digging around in a panic unable to locate her keys or wallet, as people in line behind her grew annoyed. Time after time, Jen thought, "There has to be a way to design the interior of a purse to be more functional but also fun and fashionable on the outside."

Then one day while doing dishes, Jen had an inspiration. She took the utensil holder from her dishwasher, placed it in her bag, and started filling the compartments with the contents of her purse—cell phone, cosmetics, keys, etc. No more digging. She knew instantly that this was the solution she had been searching for, and she believed that other women would feel the same. As Jen put it, "The idea worked because it was organic. I couldn't believe that nobody had figured out how to design a better handbag." Jan built a multimillion-dollar business off that one bag.

But I immediately saw that Jen had something special that went far beyond her bag. Before she invented her own product, Jen had already discovered a gift for making business happen.

Through Jen Groover Productions, she has helped clients make their dreams come true, and she has become a valuable resource for *The Big Idea*. Jen's passion and creativity are infectious. She has always been an entrepreneur, because she never wanted to be in a position where someone else could put limits on her achievements.

Jen Groover has the soul of an entrepreneur. It radiates off her—and she proves it every day. She reminds us that it really does take something special to be your own boss and create your own success. Do you have the soul of an entrepreneur? These are the qualities I believe every successful entrepreneur *must* have:

+ *You have to feel a burning desire to do something differently. Fundamentally, an entrepreneur doesn't want to play in the regular sandbox. You may appreciate that sandbox, you may like all the kids playing there, but you think maybe there's a better sandbox, or a different sandbox, or a new way to play in the sandbox. An entrepreneur is by nature a rugged individualist.*

+ *By definition, an entrepreneur is a dreamer, because what you're creating or introducing doesn't already exist anyplace in the world but in your own consciousness. You're staring at a blank page, and you're eager to fill it.*

+ *An entrepreneur must have a strong sense of self and inner fortitude. In the end, whatever product or service you're selling, you're betting on yourself. An entrepreneur has to enjoy playing without a net. I'll guarantee you that the majority of bungee jumpers are entrepreneurs. There is a lot of risk involved, and if you don't get a charge out of risk, you probably won't be a great entrepreneur.*

+ *By nature, an entrepreneur must have curiosity—a drive to explore and discover what's out there. Entrepreneurs are today's version of Ponce de Leon.*

✦ *The best entrepreneurs are people who have the ability to assemble the right group. That's the great separator at the end of the day. You can line up a hundred people who have all the other qualities, and they'll get from point A to point B. But those who get to point Z are those that have people skills. They're willing to collaborate, share, motivate, and stimulate others. They can take their personal vision and spread it around.*

Everything you do is about people. When you're hiring a manufacturer, you're not hiring a plant, you're partnering with the person running the plant. That holds true for every area of your business. Your success or failure will be determined by the team you have around you.

**BIG IDEA TOOLBOX
ENTREPRENEUR'S BOOKSHELF**

Are you ready to start carving your own path? Here are some smart choices for your bookshelf.

* *Employee to Entrepreneur: The Employee's Guide to Entrepreneurial Success,* by Suzanne Mulvehill
* *Earn What You're Worth,* by Nicole Williams
* *Zero to One Million: How I Built a Company to $1 Million in Sales,* by Ryan Allis
* *Prepare to Be a Millionaire,* by Tom Spinks, Kimberly Spinks Burleson, and Lindsay Spinks Shepherd
* *The Education of an Accidental CEO: Lessons Learned from the Trailer Park to the Corner Office,* by David Novak

When to Say "I'm Outta Here!"

Sometimes you make the move and sometimes the move makes you. Sometimes you choose to take a big risk, and sometimes you've got nothing to lose. Sometimes you quit, and sometimes you're fired.

Being fired can feel like the end of the road, but it can also be a beginning. Some of the most successful people around have been fired. I interviewed Matt Lauer, who was fired from five shows before he landed at NBC and became one of the biggest stars in television. Mike Bloomberg was fired from Salomon Brothers before he decided to make it on his own. I was fired. Being fired can be a great catalyst. It depends on your attitude. If you view yourself as a victim of circumstances beyond your control, and let bitterness overcome you, that's no good. If you walk around saying "They really screwed me," you're not going to be motivated to take a chance on a new dream. If you can see getting canned as an opportunity, you have a shot. I have always hated to fire people. I'm a real wimp about it. But usually when I do have to fire someone it's because they aren't emotionally on board. They need a push to find their passion. It's a lesson I learned from my dad.

People often ask me, "When do I know it's time to strike out on my own?" Well, you've heard the saying "Don't quit your day job." That's the ultimate risk-averse posture. There's got to be an element of risk. But in my experience, there are three circumstances that provide the perfect basis for an entrepreneurial move:

1. You have laid the groundwork.
2. You have an ideal launching pad.
3. You have nothing to lose.

1. Brick by Brick: Laying the Groundwork

I'm incredibly impressed when I meet entrepreneurs who were disciplined enough to take the long view and set the stage for their businesses over a period of years. I had a guy named John Ruf on the show. John was a UPS driver for eighteen years. During that time, he delivered thousands of gourmet food baskets and gift boxes to the customers along his route. An entrepreneur at heart, he knew that he could create a product that would appeal to both chocolate and snack lovers alike. John came up with the idea of chocolate-covered gourmet pretzels.

With two kids at home, John didn't have the luxury to quit his day job. He and his wife sat down and created a five-year plan. They trademarked their company as The Great American Pretzel Company.

In the evenings and on his days off, John started doing the research and laying the groundwork. He started small, setting up a Web site, going to trade shows, taking cell phone orders out of the back of his truck on his lunch hour.

A few years in, John and his wife attended a QVC Discovery Tour. That's where thousands of people show up, you wait in line for hours, and finally get three minutes to make your pitch. QVC called back the next day and said no, they weren't interested. But John wouldn't take no for an answer. Every month, for a year and a half, he sent a gift package to QVC, until he finally broke them down. He was in.

In the case of The Great American Pretzel Company, slow and steady won the race. John knew it was time to quit his day job when the company grew so big he could no longer do it on the side.

Big Idea Lesson: John Ruf made a five-year plan, and was patient enough to see it through. His reward was a company that was ready on day one.

2. The Right Move at the Right Time

I have a saying: "If you're making X, you're probably worth 5X." The most successful entrepreneurs are those who understand this on a gut level.

The creators of Terra Chips fit this mold. I love Terra Chips—they're a perfect party and snack food. They are the invention of two chefs, Dana Sinkler and Alex Dzieduszycki, who quit their jobs at a four-star restaurant to make it happen.

Dana and Alex were not unhappy campers. They loved their job working at Restaurant Lafayette. The motivation to form their own catering company was based on a desire to go for their worth, instead of making someone else rich. It turned out these young entrepreneurs had what it took—the vision to invent an entirely new chip. They didn't have Terra Chips in mind when they started catering. But they were open to the possibility of developing a signature hors d'oeuvre—something outside the norm of crudités and dip or the fancier foie gras. Experimenting in Alex's apartment kitchen, they created Terra Chips—multicolored sweet and savory chips made from root vegetables. Overnight, their catering clients and guests were clamoring to find out where they could buy them, and in their first year, Dana and Alex brought in a million dollars on chips alone. Eventually, they sold the business for twenty-five million dollars.

Big Idea Lesson: If you have the entrepreneurial spirit, you can find the seed for your personal potential in what you do for someone else.

3. Nothing to Lose

The reverse of laying the groundwork in a careful scheme is launching a business out of the sheer sense of having nothing to lose. That was Ramy Gafni. During the 1990s, Ramy was the hottest makeup artist in New York, working for an elite salon. His clients included luminaries such as Halle Berry, Ivanka Trump, Meredith Vieira, and Renée Zellweger. Ramy was a real creative genius, with a strong philosophy about the role of makeup. He had an idea for a line of cosmetics that would achieve maximum impact with minimum cover, and he repeatedly pitched the salon owners, urging them to develop their own line. They turned him down time and again.

Ramy still wasn't ready to jump ship and try it on his own. But an act of life intervened. In his early thirties, Ramy contracted lymphoma. While he was undergoing chemotherapy and radiation, the salon fired him. Well, cancer had toughened Ramy. He'd learned that when the shit hit the fan, he didn't have to hit it, too. Surviving lymphoma gave him a "nothing to lose" mindset. He wasn't going to curl into a ball and die. He was going to pursue his dream. He borrowed twelve thousand dollars from his parents and started Ramy Cosmetics out of his apartment. Today his company does about eleven million dollars in business. And, by the way, his old salon is closed.

> **Big Idea Lesson:** Ramy turned the worst crisis in his life into an opportunity by recognizing that he had what it took to survive anything.

BIG IDEA TOOLBOX
LEARN THE ENTREPRENEURIAL ROPES

* *Millionaire Blueprints* magazine (www.millionaireblue prints.com): Self-made millionaires show how it's done.
* Startupnation.com (www.startupnation.com): Real-world business advice for new entrepreneurs.

(continued)

- *PINK* magazine (www.pinkmagazine.com): The magazine for women in business.
- Jen Groover Productions (www.jengroover.com): Support for innovators with big ideas.
- OneCoach (www.onecoach.com): Business coaching for small businesses and start-ups.
- *Entrepreneur* magazine (www.entrepreneur.com): The leading publication for small businesses.
- Women Entrepreneurs, Inc. (www.we-inc.com): A coaching, networking, and advocacy source for women entrepreneurs.

DONNY'S DO: CONTROL, ALT, DELETE

This is a handy rubric for taking the entrepreneurial leap (based, of course, on the computer shortcut for "reset").

CONTROL: You are driven to set your own goals and expectations, not have others set them for you. Not everyone wants to be his or her own boss. Are you a person who gets a charge out of having the buck stop at your desk—for better or worse?

ALT: You're willing to risk a change in circumstances, even if it means a temporary reduction in your standard of living. Can you withstand the sacrifice it will take to get your business off the ground? Can your family?

DELETE: You're ready to leave the past behind. For most people, their workplace is their safest, most reliable community. When you leave the nest, it closes you out. It's just a fact. Are you ready to build a new nest with a new community?

CHAPTER 4

Make Love, Not
Work

Anyone who tells you that they'd rather work than make love is lying—unless their work *is* like making love. It's finding the G-spot. As I've said, the happiest people I meet are those who love what they do.

We all get a charge when these people come on the show, because they seem to have accomplished what most would think impossible. Everyone wants to know how they did it. Their stories are fun—and inspiring.

Hold Your Nose and Jump

Jeff Foxworthy has made a fortune with his "redneck" brand of comedy, which he has spun off into albums, books, movies, and television shows. It's hard to picture him sitting behind a desk at IBM, answering customer service calls, but that's what he did for five years before he even imagined himself as a comedian. He was, as he says, "just a guy in a boring job."

Jeff knew he was funny, but what could he do with that? He didn't dream about standing on a stage. But when some of his IBM coworkers urged him to enter a contest for working comics at a club near the office, he went for it. Standing on the stage, it was love at first laugh. He also won the contest. That was it for Jeff. He was quitting his day job.

"When I told my parents, they thought I was crazy," he said. "My mom was going, 'Are you on drugs? We can get you help.' I told them no, I just wanted to try this. Five years later, when I was on Johnny Carson, Mom said, 'To think you wasted five years at IBM.' "

Jeff's motivation to change his life was simple: "I didn't want to be sitting there twenty-five years later, wishing I'd tried it. I wanted to know—pass or fail—if I could do it."

One thing Jeff had going for him—which is true of every great entrepreneurial endeavor—is that he found a solid niche that wasn't being addressed by any other comedian. Redneck comedy was uncharted territory, and he saw an opportunity to validate that market through humor.

Big Idea Lesson: **Jeff found an original niche in a crowded market, and had the courage to fill it, doing what he loved.**

Jeff's wisdom, which he often preaches to his daughters, is that everyone needs to have those "hold your nose and jump" moments.

The Art of Bliss

If you look at the creators of strip cartoons, you'll notice two things: one, that they all loved drawing comics as kids, and two, they usually got serious and chose more "adult" professions when they got older. I'd guess that few career choices raise the hackles of a concerned parent like a child's announcement, "I want to be a syndicated cartoonist when I grow up." That's why most of the great cartoonists got their start in other professions.

So how did they eventually come back to follow their passion—and make millions?

We had Stephan Pastis, the creator of the cartoon strip *Pearls Before Swine,* on *The Big Idea,* and were all delighted with his story. Although Stephan had been drawing cartoons for pure pleasure since he was a kid, his grown-up job was working as an insurance lawyer in San Francisco. He hated it, but he had a family to feed, so he stuck with it.

But one day, in the midst of a particularly miserable case, Stephan seized the moment. He took a day off work and drove to Santa Rosa. Having read that the legendary *Peanuts* creator Charles Schulz ate breakfast every day at the same cafe, Stephan went there and parked himself in a booth. Sure enough, Schulz came in, sat down, and ordered breakfast. Sweating bullets and sure he'd look like a fool, Stephan went over to Schulz, got down on one knee, and said, "Mr. Schultz, I'm a lawyer . . ." Seeing Schulz's alarmed look, he immediately added, "But I draw." Schulz offered him a seat, and proceeded to spend an hour looking at Stephan's cartoons and giving him tips.

That was the emotional breakthrough for Stephan. He drove home knowing he had to do this. But it took a few more years of baby steps.

The first thing Stephan did was educate himself about the syndication business. He learned that you can't get a cartoon strip into a newspaper without going through a syndicate—there were about six of them. He bought a how-to book that advised doing a sample of about thirty strips, so he worked up four different themes with thirty strips each and sent them in. It was a high mountain to climb. Syndicates receive about six thousand submissions a year, and maybe one will be chosen. All the syndicates rejected Stephan's strips, but one thing kept him going. An editor at King Features sent a handwritten note with his rejection, telling him he had a captivating voice. That small bit of encouragement kept him going.

Stephan was determined to find out what sells. At the time, the biggest selling cartoonist was Scott Adams, creator of *Dilbert*, so on his lunch hour, Stephan would go to the local bookstore, sit on the floor, and obsessively read *Dilbert* books. It helped him learn how to write and to find his own style and rhythm.

Finally, when Stephan submitted a new strip—featuring the stick figure rat and pig that would become *Pearls Before Swine*—he got an immediate response from United Media. They signed him up to do a strip, and he was in heaven. But there was another twist. Months before the launch of his strip, as Stephan was getting ready to quit his day job, he got a call from United Media telling him that they weren't able to sell his comic. The demographic wasn't there. Stephan went from the top of the mountain to the bottom when he heard those crushing words, "You're free to go."

Just as Stephan was coming to terms with the idea that he was out of options, United Media called back. They were going to try an experiment and put his strip on their Web site—see if it got a response. It did—from the unlikeliest corner. Scott Adams himself saw the strip, liked it, and told United Media he was going to endorse it with his fans.

Big Idea Lesson: People *do* want to help—even at the risk of promoting the competition. Don't hesitate to seek out mentors.

Pearls Before Swine debuted in January 2002, and Stephan left his law firm in August of that year. Six years later, Stephan's strip is featured in 450 newspapers and he has published two book collections. But the real payoff? Happiness. As Stephan said, "My worst day as a cartoonist is better than my best day as a lawyer."

Livin' Loud

This one will blow you away. At age forty-two, Judy Davids made a career decision most girls make as teenagers. She decided to become a rock star. And that's not all. She had no training and didn't even know how to play an instrument! Yet overnight Judy went from soccer mom to rocker mom.

Judy had the vision and the passion, but how on earth did she get the gig? She started with an obvious step—taking guitar lessons during her lunch hour at work. Then, at a neighborhood barbecue, she bamboozled three moms—also possessing no experience—into starting a band with her, and the Mydols were born. Six years later, Judy

Big Idea Lesson: Be bold about following your dream. The marketplace responds to boldness.

shared their remarkable journey on *The Big Idea*. The Mydols' success was a tribute to the power of attitude and presentation. What's the first thing an aspiring rock star does? Look the part. "We believed in ourselves, and we convinced others to believe in us, too," Judy said. "We donned go-go boots and experimented with temporary hair colors. We made up some T-shirts—nothing says 'I'm a rock star' better than fluorescent T-shirts that say 'I'm a rock star'—hung up some gig posters around town, and we were on our way." They played their first gig after rehearsing just six times, advertising it as "Mom's Night Out."

The Mydols were so original, and the band's style and performances were so captivating, that the media came to them. Records, a Web site, and endorsements followed, and as one of the only mom bands in the country, they're never at a loss for gigs. Being in a rock band hasn't made them rich—yet. But the payoff is huge in other ways. Judy's message: "As long as you have passion and fun, and are constantly learning and evolving, you can do anything."

Playday to Payday

If you ask Tracy Stern what she does for a living, she'll tell you, "I play every day." Tracy has had a lifelong fascination with tea. Her passion began when she was a small child, accompanying her parents on European antique buying excursions. They encouraged her to collect teapots and cups, and she loved to dress up and host her own little tea parties. Later, while studying art and art history in Europe, Tracy found herself gravitating toward the established tearooms in Europe and Asia. When she returned to Tampa, she opened a tearoom inspired by the seventeenth-century French salons. After that, the next step was creating her own signature teas—whimsical, elegant, and totally original blends that have signature identities. They include The Musician (rooibos blended with hibiscus and rose petals), The Writer (Indian chai tea with cardamom, cloves, and cinnamon), and The Romantic (Chur She green tea with jasmine flowers).

Big Idea Lesson: Behind every product is a pleasure principle. By exploiting her childhood fantasies to evoke the exotic, glamorous flavor of the European salon, Tracy brought her product to an American market.

Today SalonTea is a fast-growing global business, bringing in $1.5 million a year.

"I know I'm supposed to be a grown-up," Tracy laughed when she came on *The Big Idea*. "But I'm like a child having a tea party every day."

**THE MILLIONAIRE PASSION TEST:
ARE YOU REALLY DOING
WHAT YOU LOVE?**

Are you ready to do what you love AND make millions? Take
this test and find out.

1. As a kid, what did you want to be when you grew up?
2. More importantly, why? What emotional need did that
   dream satisfy?
3. Does that emotional connection exist in your current job?
   How?
4. What gives you a high? If you had three hours to do
   anything, what would you do?
5. How could you translate that into making your millions?
   What kind of business could fulfill your emotional need?
   (Make a list.)

BOTTOM LINE: You need to find a way to use your adult interests and skills to satisfy your oldest emotional needs. It may
take trial and error, but there is a path for you that can com-
bine them all. If you can focus in on your passions in life, and
have the motivation to follow them, you are already on the
road to the American dream!

The Power of Nostalgia

Do you have a yearning for something more in your life, but
aren't sure what it is or where to take it? Are you ready to tap
into that place of pure childhood pleasure—and make a living
in the process? How do you start? Take a trip down memory

lane to a scene in your childhood where you can visualize your-self being happy.

Rick Field worked in television for fifteen years, and hit a wall when he was turning forty. It just wasn't doing it for him any-more. Rick had always held on to the happy memory of his child-hood, when his family would spend summers in Vermont making pickles. Uncertain what direction his life would take, he started making pickles in his New York City apartment—in part to re-capture the feelings he'd had as a child, and in part because he just loved pickles. It went from a casual activity to a serious hobby to an obsession—and finally, a business, Rick's Picks. The turning point was winning the 2001 National Pickle Festival Best in Show. Five years later, Rick had moved from his kitchen to a fac-tory, and was overseeing a network of regional producers. The wake-up call for Rick was the recognition that the happiest times of his childhood could liter-ally become his adult reality.

Big Idea Lesson: Childhood dreams are the incubators for adult success.

In every flush of nostal-gia, there is a gold nugget of truth. The first time I did tele-vision, I felt a jolt of pleasurable recognition. Where had I felt that rush before? Looking back, I saw myself at age fifteen in my tenth-grade speech class. Man, I loved that class. It was the only one I looked forward to. It didn't feel like school; it was fun. I'd write speeches and get up and have a ball delivering them with drama and humor. I'd have the class in the palm of my hand, and it felt great. That was the real me—being able to use my mind, my voice, my passion to evoke an emotional response in others. And now I get to do it every day on *The Big Idea*.

DONNY'S DO: LOVER'S LEAP

In our buttoned-up, boxed-in society, the idea of choosing a career based on love sounds like madness—as crazy as taking a leap off a high bridge. But one thing I've learned, from my own experience and talking to other wildly successful and wildly happy people, is that it's not that scary and it's not that crazy. People who talk about walking into their boss's office and quitting to pursue their dreams describe being instantly elated and secure in the decision, even when they have only two nickels to rub together. I rarely hear anyone say, "Oh, my God, what have I done?" They just know it's right. I believe that there's a place inside each person where you *know* what you should be doing. Then it's just a matter of taking the leap.

There Are No Geniuses

CHAPTER 5

There's Gotta Be a
Better Way

What's bugging you? And what are you going to do about it?

You are surrounded by everyday obstacles that frustrate and annoy you—things that waste your time and cause you unnecessary stress. You have two choices . . . you can muddle through, or you can say: "There's gotta be a better way—and *I'm* going to find it."

The urge to make life better has been a consistent theme of human history. It's the most fundamental catalyst for action. It goes to the core of human drive and intelligence. Without this urge to improve, there would be no automobiles, airplanes, or computers. For that matter, there would also be no toilet paper rolls, hair clips, or drinking straws. Once a better way enters the public arena, there's no going back. Can you imagine buying a car without cup holders?

No one ever made millions by leaving well enough alone. It's so simple sometimes, it boggles my mind, but I see it time and again. Bright, aware, creative individuals find a niche that's not being filled or a way to solve a nagging problem. As the saying goes, if you build a better mousetrap, the world will beat a path to your door. The trick is spotting that opportunity.

Million-dollar ideas are literally everywhere, waiting for someone to stumble upon them. Once you start thinking about your daily life this way, you'll see it, too.

The take-home message is that you don't have to come up with something entirely novel or hugely complex for it to be a winning innovation. You can zero in on the most minute element. You can't let the thought that "this is too simple, this is too easy" stop you from really pursuing an idea you believe in. Most of the time, when an idea or a product is just "too simple" or "too easy" and it's not already out there, you've got yourself a million-dollar idea!

This driving concept is a cornerstone of *The Big Idea*. I love it when these people come on my show, because they turned frustration into business gold. They achieved something exquisitely simple: They solved a personal problem. In this complex, technological world, not every idea is simple, of course. But the ideas that really resonate with me are those that immediately evoke a big "Duh!"

Feel the Need

During more than twenty-five years in advertising, it became second nature for me to look for the human, emotional connection between a product and its audience. The market is not an abstract entity that you have to wow with your creative genius. It's real people with desires and needs. The job is to show them that you have the product or service that adds value to their lives. If a product doesn't meet a need, all the marketing in the world can't sell it. Remember the great fiasco of the New Coke? Why did it fail? It didn't fail because it was a lousy product, although there's some debate about that. It failed for a simple reason: It was attempting to solve a problem that didn't exist. People liked the old Coke just fine.

The need can be utterly mundane. In fact, those are the best ideas, in my opinion. We had Sara Blakely, the creator of Spanx, on the show. Spanx is a phenomenally successful innovation in women's undergarments, doing about $200 million in business. Oprah swears by it. Tyra loves it. But it started from the smallest place. Seven years ago, Sara was selling faxes and copy machines door to door and trying to decide what she was going to do with her life. She'd always dreamed of being a lawyer, but she'd flunked the LSAT tests, so she knew she had to find another dream. In the scheme of things, visible panty lines wasn't her biggest problem, but it was bugging her. One night, she had the inspiration to cut the feet off her panty hose to wear with white pants and open-toed shoes. It worked great, and an idea was born.

With five thousand dollars in savings, Sara set out to bring her idea into being. She went to North Carolina and started driving from mill to mill, looking for someone who would agree to manufacture her product. She got shut out time after time. None of these guys got it. But finally a mill owner who had turned her down initially, called and said he'd changed his mind. When she asked him why, he said, "I have two daughters." Which just goes to show that if you hit the right target, you'll get a response.

Once she had a prototype, Sara called the buyer at Neiman Marcus and said she'd fly to Dallas if the buyer would give her ten minutes. The buyer agreed, and Sara proceeded to make the most shameless and effective pitch she could think of. I love this—it's pure ingenuity. She took the buyer into the ladies' room and personally demonstrated the before and after in her cream pants. Three weeks later, Spanx was on the shelves at Neiman Marcus.

That's the short version of Sara's story. In all, it's taken seven years to become the incredible success story she is today. But the origins of Spanx were simple, obvious, and solved a problem every woman has.

Let me tell you one more thing about Sara that is absolutely key to her success. She wasn't afraid to fail. Listen up, parents—because this is a lesson she learned from childhood.

Big Idea Lesson: If you can solve a problem that is common for any group of people, you can make millions.

Sara's father was a remarkable guy. Once a week at the dinner table, he would ask his kids, "What did you fail at today?" Sara learned from an early age that failure was just the means of nudging you in a different direction. If she'd passed the LSAT, she wouldn't be where she is today. She can easily see that failure as a lucky break.

TAKE ACTION ON YOUR DREAMS FROM START-UP NATION'S RICH AND JEFF SLOAN

STEP 1: Take a snapshot of your current life. Rate your life on a scale of one to a hundred. Ninety percent of people probably are NOT where they want to be.

STEP 2: Paint the picture of how big your life can be. Make a bulleted list of what you want your life to be. The sky is the limit. Factor in things like family time, hobbies, charity work, and early retirement.

STEP 3: Define your passions. Think about the types of things that you love to do—whether at work, at home, or at your local soup kitchen. List them.

STEP 4: Define your strengths and accomplishments. List the abilities, experience, and strengths you can build on to get your ideal life. Bear in mind that your skills need not be strictly from your professional life. List the skills developed in your personal life as well.

STEP 5: Think about your ideal work style. Whether full-time or part-time, at-home or on the road, working behind the scenes or interacting with lots of people—understand what your work style priorities are so you can define the best kind of business for you.

STEP 6: Write your manifesto. This is your personal mission, your values, and what drives you forward, all wrapped up into a one-page (maximum) statement. To write this, you should draw on everything you've already discovered about yourself in steps one through five, and bring it all together into a clear statement of your principles and priorities.

For more, go to www.startupnation.com.

Five Steps to a Better Way

Do you want to join the millionaires' club by introducing a better way to the world? Here's my formula—with examples that will really wake you up to the possibilities. I promise you'll be inspired by the simplicity of their solutions—and the guts it took to make them a reality.

My better way formula has five basic points:

1. **Acknowledge it.**
2. **Own it.**
3. **Make it.**
4. **Wear it.**
5. **Sell it.**

Let's dig deeper.

1. Acknowledge It.

There's a saying in self-help circles that the first step to solving a problem is acknowledging that you have one. That's also the best wisdom when it comes to developing a new product. Everybody's got problems—find yours and turn it into gold.

Here's an example of a consumer problem that is universal: keeping cereal, chips, and other dry goods fresh once you open the package. Am I right? Well, one mother took it to the next level. Denise Bein said, "I'm tired of throwing away stale food, and I'm not going to take it anymore." She sat down at her kitchen table and created a package seal that could fit on the top of any box or bag, using half of a Ziploc bag with adhesive on the bottom and a resealable opening on top.

Denise had never made or marketed a product before, but that didn't stop her. She put together a bunch of samples and started handing them out to her friends. The response was overwhelmingly positive. Finally, a friend said, "I love it. What are you going to do with this idea?"

Denise replied, "I'm going to find out how to do it." And just like that, she was committed, and she never looked back. With extensive research and the support of an inventors' association in Arizona, Denise found a way to produce a product that revolutionized the pantry.

Big Idea Lesson: No matter how many thousands of products are on the market, there's *always* room for a better way.

Here's one you'll love. A problem every human being has that's a little delicate. Luc Galbert came on the show to discuss his solution to this unmentionable, but very real issue, bathroom smells. The idea came to him when he was at his mother-in-law's house and he had to go. With no air fresheners in sight, he considered locking himself in the bathroom until he died of embarrassment. In that moment, Luc had an inspiration: "Everybody's gotta go." What if it was possible to eliminate bath-room smells altogether—not just cover them up with floral scents, but get rid of them?

Over the next year, Luc researched the problem, and ulti-mately aligned himself with an Asian manufacturer who devised a natural, nontoxic formula, which he called Just a Drop. The idea was to squirt a single drop into the toilet before you go, and, like magic—no bad smells.

Luc tested his product by starting with everyone he knew. He gave bottles to his doctor, dentist, friends, neighbors—and the response was beyond enthusiastic. "Women especially were clamoring for it," he said. "They told me it was better than mar-riage counseling."

Just a Drop is a no-brainer solution. There's no question in my mind that Luc will make millions with his product. He's already sold 600,000 units online and through Wal-Mart in Canada. All because he had a mo-ment of embarrassment, and decided to make it go away for good.

> **Big Idea Lesson: If you think you've found a better way, your most effective test market is the people you know.**

2. Own It.

If you see a need and have an idea how to meet it, don't assume that someone else has done it. I've heard people put down their own great ideas, saying, "It's so obvious, I'm sure it's out there. I just haven't found it yet." Chances are, if you don't see it, it doesn't exist. But test the premise. Do your research. Get on the Internet and do a market and patent search. Get out in the world and look for it. Go to the customer service counter at Costco or Bed, Bath & Beyond or Home Depot, and say, "I'm looking for an item that does x, y, z." In the course of your research, maybe you'll find a similar product that doesn't quite solve the problem to your satisfaction. Or maybe you'll find a big zero—which means the universe is wide-open for you to step in.

When Christine Ingemi, the creator of iHearSafe earbuds, went to electronics stores to buy a product that would automatically set earphone volume at a lower decibel, she was shocked to find that no such product existed. As the mother of four kids who were constantly plugged into their iPods, Christine was very concerned about the long-term effects of high volumes on their tender ears. Like many parents, she had read the alarming studies about the damage that could be caused by the constant bombardment of sound. She'd tried the parental control volume limiters, but her kids were magicians with the reset button.

When Christine discovered there was no fail-proof product that lowered earphone volume, she could have walked away and said, "I hope someone comes up with this product before my kids blow their eardrums out." She could have prayed to the gods of product development to please deliver a solution. Or she could have confiscated the iPods. Instead, she decided to make it herself.

Now, you've got to know how amazing that is. Christine and her husband, Rick, had a gumball vending machine business in New Hampshire. They knew nothing about technology, and they weren't plugged into the network.

So they threw themselves into learning. They interviewed dozens of experts in product development and patenting. They hooked up with audiologists and scientists who could guarantee a high-quality product. The result, iHearSafe earbuds, looks like any standard pair of earbuds with two small earphones that fit snugly in the ears, but with one difference. A small volume-reducing circuit that prevents sounds from exceeding eighty-five decibels—the level deemed safe by audiologists—is placed in the length of the earbud wire.

The next step was getting the product in front of the right audience. This is a good example of amateur moxie. Christine heard about a noise-induced hearing loss convention in Kentucky. What better place for her to demonstrate her product, right? She hopped on a plane and showed up at the site, only to be told she couldn't get in the door because she wasn't registered. "I wasn't going to let that stop me," she said. She marched over to a nearby shoeshine stand and paid the guy fifty dollars to let her set up a demonstration. She was positioned directly in the line of sight for conventiongoers entering and exiting their meetings. "I made a lot of noise that day," she said. And she kept on making noise. Christine literally invented a new category in a market that is growing bigger every day.

Big Idea Lesson: **You don't have to be a technical expert to invent a new technology. The idea is the key. Then seek out people who know how to do it.**

PROTECT YOUR BIG IDEA

A key aspect of "owning" it is to make it official. If your invention is truly original, protect it with a patent. A patent is the grant of a property right to the inventor, issued by the United States Patent and Trademark Office. The process can be complicated and lengthy, so it's wise to seek the services of a patent attorney. The USPTO has an excellent Web site (www.uspto.gov) that details everything you need to know to get started.

What does a patent provide? A patent gives you the right to exclude others from making, using, offering for sale, or selling the invention in the United States or importing the invention into the United States.

(continued)

What is a provisional patent? A provisional application for a patent is a lower cost filing that allows the inventor to use the term "patent pending." It is a way to temporarily protect your invention until you're ready to submit a full application.

What is a trademark? A trademark is your identity mark—a name, logo, or symbol that sets your business apart. By registering your trademark, you go on record as the owner.

3. Make It.

If you have a big idea for a new product that you think can earn you millions, the first step is to take it out of your head and figure out how to make it.

If your idea is simple, you can sit down and create a prototype. I get a lot of people on the show who have made prototypes out of cardboard, glue, paper bags, drinking straws, pieces of plastic, hair pins—you name it. It's wild. Sophistication goes out the window. The important thing is that you have to be able to prove that your product works.

Lisa Lloyd, a dynamic young entrepreneur, came on the show and blew us all away with the simplicity of her process. Lisa invented the French Twister, a hair clip that makes it easy to make a French twist, even if your hair is short. Lisa was a single mom making thirteen thousand dollars a year selling ad space, so she was starting at zero. She experimented with common items, cutting up toilet paper rolls, bending hairpins, molding little pieces of plastic until she had the right model. It was a bare bones operation.

Lisa experimented with various plastics until she found one that felt right. She kept improving on the design until she knew she had the perfect clip.

Now, the question was, how to get her hair clip manufactured? She sold her old car for five hundred dollars, borrowed two hundred dollars from her mom, and found a local plastics molding shop through a library search. After five hundred units were produced, Lisa went to salons. The product proved to be a hit with the salon clients. Why? It worked. An instant way to look glamorous, no matter what kind of hair you have. What's not to love?

When you invent a new product, you have to decide whether you're going to produce and market it yourself, partner with a manufacturer, or make a licensing deal with an existing company. Lisa wanted to make a licensing deal, but she knew nothing about barrette companies. So she did the obvious thing—she went to the stores and started looking at the names on the packages of barrettes. One she liked, Scunci, had the address and telephone number right on the package. She decided to give them a call. It was just before Christmas, and Scunci was closed, but a guy answered the phone. No, it wasn't the custodian. It was the owner, who was there to work in peace and quiet. He listened to Lisa's story, and the beginnings of a deal were made that day.

Big Idea Lesson: **If your friends are telling you they love the way you do something— whether it's how you fix your hair or how you bake your brownies— you could be sitting on a million-dollar idea.**

The French Twister changed Lisa's life. With an overall investment of less than a thousand dollars, she created a product that has done thirty million dollars in retail sales.

4. Wear It.

Your best test market is your own backyard. Alicia Shaffer, founder of the Peanut Shell Baby Sling, found success by taking her creation and wearing it in public. Alicia was a brand-new mom who wanted to keep her baby close but still be able to use her hands, take walks, and do the stuff she needed to do. She tried various baby slings that were on the market, but found them either too cumbersome, too uncomfortable, or too unfashionable. She wanted a stylish baby sling that would look and feel great, and it just wasn't out there. So she decided to do her own version. She cut up a bedsheet, took it to a local seamstress, and created a comfortable, good-looking sling. "I made it for me," she told me. "I wasn't thinking about a product." But then she wore it to her mommy groups, and she was bombarded. "I love it . . . Where did you get it? . . . Will you make me one just like it?" She made ten more for other mothers, then ten more, then ten more. Literally, baby steps.

Alicia and her husband decided to produce the product, naming it Peanut Shell after the nickname they gave their baby.

By the time Alicia came on *The Big Idea*, she had a small business going. Now she wanted to take it to the next level, and her appearance caught the attention of a rep who worked with the buyers at Babies "R" Us. Within a few weeks they were doing business with Babies "R" Us online, and soon after that they were in the stores.

Big Idea Lesson: If you've got it, flaunt it. By wearing her creation in public, Alicia made an impact that snowballed into a ten-million-dollar business.

It all goes to show that friends and family are your best advertising and marketing tool. But having celebrities on board doesn't hurt either. When a celebrity is about to have a baby, Alicia makes it a point to send a Peanut Shell. High-profile fans include Brooke Shields, Heidi Klum, Denise Richards, Gwen Stefani, and Marcia Cross.

And we can't talk about *wearing it* without mentioning Scott Jordan. Scott was just another overworked lawyer who wasn't thrilled with his job. He wasn't necessarily looking for a big idea—but one came along and bit him. Scott was a gadget guy, but his gadgets were driving him crazy. His iPod cord was always tangled. His cell phone was never within easy reach. He had too much to carry. So Scott asked himself, "What if I could *wear* my gear?"

In 2001, using his savings, Scott quit his job at a mega law firm and created Gear Management Solution, with the idea of developing technology-enabled clothing. His concept was a vest or jacket that could hold, without bulging, all the equipment of modern life. Scott had no experience making products, so he hired a team of designers and engineers to give him expert advice. He was most interested in learning about the common devices people carry and how they used them. He realized that his invention had to give people easy access to their devices, yet keep them from bulging out of pockets. Scott didn't want his clothing to look unattractive or "geeky." He was looking for a sleek design, something that could be appealing to a variety of customers, from businesspeople to students.

The result was the SCOTTEVEST, which he demonstrated on *The Big Idea*. Scott's jacket looked sleek and stylish, so we were all pretty amazed when he began to unload stuff from its twenty-two hidden pockets. What an invention!

Wearing his vest on *The Big Idea* paid off for Scott and got him attention from one of his idols, Steve Wozniak, the cofounder of Apple. Wozniak e-mailed Scott and blew his mind with his enthusiastic words:

"I speak about the Apple story, but yours is much more relevant for all the budding entrepreneurs out there. Everywhere I go there are dozens or hundreds of hungry faces of people who would love to hear your story. I do love my Scott products but don't [yet] use them enough. I'm so constantly busy that I don't even have my clothes in a closet but in piles on my floor (my eVests are hanging, though). My son has worn your vest for years and everywhere he goes he has everything. He does have fun in airports! I am a true fan of yours and am going to send that video to my list. I can't tell you how proud I am just to know you! Highest regards, Woz."

It all goes to show—wear it and they will come!

5. Sell It.

Before the world can beat a path to your door, you have to let it know you're out there. A lot of people choke at the point of selling an idea, especially if they've always been shy. You don't have to be especially charismatic or gregarious to make the sale. You just have to believe in your product.

Never forget, buyers are people too. They have the same issues everyone has. If you appeal to the emotional need, you can get a foot in the door.

Consider how you can make that personal connection. Remember Sara Blakely's bathroom demonstration? She got lucky because the Neiman Marcus buyer was a woman. But Sara took it to the next level. She appealed to her as a person who might need the product herself. (I'd be willing to bet that that first buyer wears Spanx today.)

Buyers like to be part of a new wave, but you have to show them you're willing to share the risk. You can't just say, "Here's my product. I believe it will sell. Good luck." Don't leave them shouldering all the risk. Alicia Shaffer did a smart thing with the Peanut Shell Baby Sling. She took it to local baby boutiques and told them, "If it doesn't sell in two weeks, we'll buy it back from you." She made them partners in the sales process—and it paid off for her.

Denise Bein, the creator of Quick Seals, ran up against a huge barrier when she tried to get her product into chains. She had no trouble making the sale. The buyers loved the product and wanted to sign her up. The problem came when they sent her the contracts and she learned about slotting fees. Slotting fees are an upfront display charge—all the stores have them. When Denise realized it could cost her twenty to fifty thousand dollars per chain just to get in the stores, she was shocked. She didn't have that kind of money, and it could have been a deal breaker. But instead of folding up her tent and slinking off into oblivion, she found a better way to display her product. She developed a Try Me Pack that hung on clip strips that could be placed anywhere in a store. No slotting fee. She was in. There is always another way.

> **Big Idea Lesson:** If in your heart you truly believe that your product is a better way, you won't take no for an answer. You'll keep pounding on the door until the right person responds.

DONNY'S DO: THE INSTANT GRAB

Every day on the show we look at new products and ask, "Is this a million-dollar idea?" We review hundreds of tapes, looking for that instant grab—the idea that we get right away. The best are those that can be described in a single sentence. We're going to talk later about making a perfect pitch, but one thing is clear: If you can't describe your product in one sentence, you need to go back to the drawing board. Why? Because the big idea that truly grabs people is going to elicit an immediate, visceral reaction.

We ask our guests to finish the line "There's gotta be a better way to . . ." Here are some clear pitches from people on our show:

"There's gotta be a better way to . . . eliminate bathroom odors" (Just a Drop odor neutralizer).

"There's gotta be a better way to . . . slice bagels without losing a finger" (The Bagel Guillotine).

"There's gotta be a better way to . . . conceal bra straps" (Strap Tamers).

"There's gotta be a better way to . . . eliminate visible panty lines" (Spanx).

In every case, the market pitch is short and straightforward. It hits a bull's-eye.

CHAPTER **6**

Why Didn't **I** Think of That?

t's staring you in the face. It's knocking you on the head. It's so obvious, you can't believe that you never thought of it. But you didn't, and someone else did—and they're making millions.

So what's the difference between the people rising to the top and the people slapping themselves on the head? Let's take a look at some of the deciding factors. They include:

A moment of clarity

A new twist

A captive market

A future vision

A Moment of Clarity

The big ideas have always been out there, but it takes a moment of clarity to actually realize the hidden potential. That's when you internalize the need and realize that you can be the one to do something about it. The moment of clarity is the launchpad for your idea, and it usually comes in the most mundane setting.

Jill Starishevsky was a nine-year veteran of the district attorney's office in New York City, where she prosecuted sex crimes and child abuse. She was also a mother of two, so her antennae were out the day she took her lunch break in a local park. She noticed two young girls playing on the jungle gym. Jill watched as the little girls approached a woman who was reading a book. She appeared to be their nanny, but she wasn't paying attention. As she finished her lunch, Jill continued to keep an eye out for the girls, worried that they might wander off or even run into the street. As a district attorney, she understood how quickly a disaster could strike when kids are left unsupervised. She would have liked to let the children's parents know about the nanny's inattention, but she didn't know how to reach them.

Jill was a working mother herself, and she knew that she'd want to know if her own nanny was being neglectful. And that's how she came up with the idea of HowsMyNanny. Parents register at the Web site and receive a small license plate that is attached to a stroller. People who observe bad (or good) nanny behavior can report anonymously to the site, and parents are notified.

So, did Jill's moment of clarity launch a million-dollar business? On the show, we gave her suggestions about how to grow her business, including engaging with nanny agencies and creating bumper magnets for cars. Jill is making inroads through lots of media publicity and partnering up with groups that share her passion for protecting kids. I think this is a winner—and it all started with a moment of clarity.

Big Idea Lesson: See it and do it. If you can imagine a need, you can be the one to find a way to meet it.

Brian Quittner's moment of clarity came on the job. Brian was a fourteen-year veteran of the Santa Barbara Harbor Patrol, work that could be dangerous—and dark. He always carried a flashlight, and when he needed to use both hands, he tucked it under his arm. One night while he was writing a citation, his flashlight slipped and smashed on the ground, leaving him in the dark.

A lightbulb went on over Brian's head. He needed a reliable hands-free light source. Back at the station, Brian sketched a prototype for a lightweight, hands-free device that could fit into a uniform shirt pocket. His invention contained some enhancements that he knew would benefit his colleagues—such as an adjustable light arm and battery-saving features. And, of course, he had to make sure that his design would not impede night vision.

Big Idea Lesson: Start with a specific, targeted need, and then grow it forward. Brian's QuiqLite idea did exactly that.

The initial response to Brian's invention, which he called the QuiqLite, was so enthusiastic that he knew he had a business opportunity. Within a short time, he and his wife Rachel were filling orders from all over the globe, using their living room as a base.

Brian's initial vision was to produce a light that would fit the needs of others like himself. He never imagined it would benefit such a diverse group of people. Today, QuiqLite is used by thousands in virtually all sectors, from police departments to industry, airlines to multiple branches of government. It's also popular with outdoorsmen and students.

Brian's success with QuiqLite has led him to other inventions, such as Night Nurse, a hands-free light source for professionals in the healthcare industry, and for those getting up at night with an infant, QuiqLite Babeebrite.

A New Twist

Every commodity currently on sale is a new opportunity, if you can find that special twist. David Roth and Rick Bacher have done that with their brilliant concept, Cereality. Cereal is a staple of American life. Nothing new about that. What's new about Cereality is that David and Rick took the product and found a way to capture the lifestyle—what they call "the Saturday morning experience." They created a retail cereal bar where customers could choose from over thirty cereals and forty toppings and have them served up in any combination by pajama-clad employees—Wheaties with Fruity Pebbles, Froot Loops with Cocoa Puffs, cornflakes with Grape-Nuts, and everything in between. This "home for cereal away from home" gets at the ritual of eating cereal and the role this experience plays in American life.

The first Cereality was opened in 2003 near the University of Arizona campus—a great target market—and has since opened three additional outlets, with twenty-six franchises under contract. It's such a great idea that others have tried to copy it, but David and Rick have been very aggressive about trademarking to protect their idea. The best protection, though—just to grow.

Big Idea Lesson: **Promote the lifestyle, not the product. What is the human longing you're responding to?**

I think Cereality is a home run in the manner of Starbucks—making something new from an existing product, understanding the emotional need of the customer, and creating a lifestyle experience.

Michael Kirban and Ira Liran found a new twist by figuring out a way to take a Brazilian staple and bring it to America. I liked this story because not only were they wildly successful, but their idea had its origins in a most seductive setting. I'm a sucker for a good boy-meets-girl-meets-big-idea story!

Michael and Ira were hanging out in a bar in New York City, chatting up two girls from Brazil. When they asked the girls what they missed most from their native country, the response was instantaneous: "*Agua de coco*." The girls raved about their favorite native drink.

Fast-forward a year and Ira married one of the Brazilian girls. He followed her to Brazil, where he discovered the truth of her earlier declaration. Coconut water was huge. People couldn't get enough of it. He called his friend Michael, still in New York, and they began to hatch a plan for bringing it to the United States. They knew it would be a hard sell because Americans just didn't drink the stuff. As Ira worked the product development end in Brazil, Michael started pitching retailers. The plan was to sell Vita Coco coconut water as "a vacation in a bottle." At first, the response was negative. "One retailer said, 'This tastes like sock water,'" Michael told me.

Success ultimately came when they stopped selling a dream and started selling functionality. Their product had the makings of a powerful sports drink. It was loaded with electrolytes, potassium, and minerals. Michael began pitching the drink as a natural rehydrant, and made the first big sale to Whole Foods. Today, Vita Coco coconut water is in five thousand U.S. stores, gyms, cafes, and juice bars. Sales reached four million dollars last year.

Big Idea Lesson: It's a small world, after all. If you find the right twist, an international best seller can become a national favorite.

Behind every new idea is an age-old need. If you're thinking, "What a great idea!" there's a chance others have had the same inspiration. Before you do anything else, start with research. Some of the most successful businesses are twists on old ideas. For example, people have been making and selling pretzels since the Middle Ages, but look how many new pretzel companies have been started in the last couple of decades.

A Captive Market

I'm always amazed by how many times people answer the question "Who's your market?" with "Well, everyone." You may think your target market is the world, but the most successful businesses are those that find a captive market niche. You can always expand once you're up and running. I've been impressed by entrepreneurs who recognized a narrow niche and designed a product or service to fit, then were able to broaden it to other categories.

One of the most captive markets resides on college campuses. College kids are the ultimate consumers, they respond to lifestyle pitches, and they're willing to pay for it. It's striking how many great ideas are launched to the college market.

The kernel of Brian Altomare's idea for a business that moved kids in and out of college dorms was born from his own experience. When he started college, he had a ton of stuff to cart to his dorm. Brian's parents packed their car to the brim, only to have it blow out a tire on the freeway. Just one more stressful, horrendous college move, out of many thousands happening simultaneously all over the country. As he sat miserably by the side of the road waiting for the repair truck, Brian was fantasizing about his stuff being magically transported to his dorm room. But the idea for MadPackers didn't actually gel until four years later, when Brian, a newly minted college grad, started thinking about what he was going to do with his life. That's when he got serious about an idea that had been rolling around in his head since that fateful freeway blowout—an easy way to move college kids and their stuff in and out of dorms.

He devised the name MadPackers and paid a college kid to design a Web site. Then he started cold-calling schools to pitch the idea.

Big Idea Lesson: Don't start out selling to the world. Sell to your own neighborhood, and the world will follow.

Everyone loved it, but they were reluctant to support Brian's plan until he had an actual shipping infrastructure in place. That problem was solved when Universal Express, a luggage shipping company, agreed to partner with him. From there MadPackers took off, with a captive market to the tune of almost two million dollars a year—so far.

A Future Vision

By nature, a new invention is inspired by a vision of the future. As Noel Lee, creator of Monster Cable, discovered, every revolutionary idea predates the public awareness of a need. In 1978, Noel was a laser-fusion design engineer at Lawrence Livermore National Laboratory in San Francisco. He was also a drummer with the band Asian Wood and a devoted audiophile, always looking for ways to improve sound quality. The innovation that produced Monster Cable came from Lee's realization that not all wires are equal when it comes to audio performance. His high-performance speaker cable improved performance when hooked up to loudspeakers, and they were a huge success.

But it didn't happen overnight. The world wasn't demanding a new cable, and Noel was faced with every visionary's dilemma—convincing people they needed something that they didn't know they needed. "I had a product nobody wanted," Noel told us on *The Big Idea*. "Who needs a better wire?"

Noel knew that in order to make headway, he had to take his cable to the Consumer Electronics Show. So off he went, driving to Chicago with nothing but cardboard boxes and a paper bag full of his Monster Cables. He was able to borrow a portion of an existing booth to demonstrate his product next to standard speaker cables. The interest was middling. Noel was still ahead of his time. Monster's big break didn't come until the next CES, when he got a monster order—30,000 cables—which he had

Big Idea Lesson: **If your vision is revolutionary, the world will catch up—eventually.** trouble filling. His success took him by surprise. With direct access to people he would never meet otherwise, CES gave Noel and his small company endless opportunities. Now Monster remains a privately held company, with annual revenues around five hundred million dollars.

Will Your Idea Make Millions?

Do you have a fire in the belly to bring your idea to the world? That's a great first step. But before you charge ahead, you'll need to come back down to earth and find out if your idea passes the business success test. Let's do a little reality check, starting with some fundamental questions.

One segment on *The Big Idea* is called "Minutes to Millions." We bring on an entrepreneur who is convinced that his or her product will make millions, and then ask a panel, composed of people who have succeeded in doing just that, to judge it against a ticking clock. When we first started planning this segment, we decided to focus on four tangible elements of every successful product, asking:

Does it have a million-dollar name?
Does it have million-dollar packaging?
Does it have a million-dollar price point?
Does it have a million-dollar market?

Let's examine why these factors can make or break your product launch.

THE NAME: How important is a name? I don't think you can ever say that a name makes or breaks a product. If it's a fantastic product, a lousy name won't sink it. If it's a lousy product, a great name won't sell it. But you can move people with a name. You can make an aspirational statement that draws in an audience. You can appeal to an audience's curiosity, as Google did. Sometimes you can own a category with a name, as Noel Lee did with Monster Cable.

Make sure your name reflects the style and mood of your product. One of our "Minutes to Millions" guests was the inventor of Flexflops, a super cute portable flip-flop. We loved the product, and we thought it was a million-dollar idea. But I felt the name was too utilitarian. It needed to be cheekier.

Another product, also a winner that needed work on the name, was The Original Runner Company. What do you think of when you see the word *runner*? Running shoes, sports gear—right? But this product has nothing to do with running. It's a customized, fabric wedding aisle runner. It just didn't come through with the name.

When you're picking a name, do a trademark and title search. That's obvious. But don't forget to do an Internet domain name search at the same time. For many businesses today, trade names are synonymous with domain names—such as Amazon.com and Monster.com. Domain names are not registered through state or local government; rather they can be obtained through numerous online businesses, most of which will allow you to conduct a name search prior to purchase to make sure your chosen name isn't taken.

NAMES THAT NAIL IT

CLEARLY DEFINES THE PRODUCT:
The Wing Zone
Quick Seals

(continued)

Strap Tamers
Rent-A-Husband

HIP AND COOL:
Tarte cosmetics
Bear Naked Granola

ALL-AMERICAN APPEAL:
The Great American Pretzel Company
Omaha Steaks
Sam Adams beer

THE PACKAGE: Your package is your calling card. It's one of the most important marketing decisions you'll ever make. Here's where you have to "get" your customer. A package is not an inert thing—it's a living representation of your product. The look of your package has to be targeted to the people who will find it appealing—whether that appeal is beauty, hipness, warmth, technology, glamour, or practicality. That being said, there are some basic rules. First and foremost: Show the product.

We live in an environment where less is more. People today are ultra-sensitive about eliminating waste, and minimal packaging is in. We liked the way SingleTease—T-shirts with conversation starters like "Just ask me . . . out"—accomplished this with a provocative hang-tag that got the message across with a few words. Not every product has that option. But when it comes to packaging, simpler is better.

When you're designing your package, think about what draws you to take a second look. And conversely, what frustrates you? The best packaging answers the questions of functionality and style. And if it's a "Try Me" product—like an electronic device—you need to allow for that in the packaging. Remember the hugely successful Tickle Me Elmo? One key to its success was that customers could reach right through the package to make Elmo laugh.

THE PRICE: Many of the new businesspeople we see on the show come at pricing with dread. They feel as if they're entering a foreign territory where the rules are not clear. They're afraid they'll price too high and sacrifice sales, or more alarming, price too low and miss out on profits. Obviously, the first rule of business is that you have to make a profit. You can give some things away for free; you just can't give *everything* away for free.

There are a multitude of factors to consider when choosing a price: Your production and operating costs, the price point of similar products, and the nature of your market. But surprisingly, the biggest mistake people make is underpricing. Once you set your price, it is very hard to raise it, whereas if you set your price too high, you can always lower it.

The main selling point of your product will help to determine your price point. If you're marketing luxury, a discount price will drive away customers. If you're marketing convenience, you have some flexibility, as many people will pay more for convenience. If you're marketing to a teen or 'tween crowd, you have to take the price down.

If you've been alive on the planet for more than five minutes, you already know that $19.99 is a more appealing discount price than $20. Why? Because the first number you see is *one*, not *two*. But what if you're trying to communicate luxury? Then $19.99 feels cheap.

Again, do your research. If you're selling an electronic item, camp out in an electronics store. If you're selling shoes, hang out in the shoe department. Find out what people are actually paying for products in your category.

THE MARKET: Nine out of ten entrepreneurs we feature on our "Minutes to Millions" segment begin by defining a market that is much too broad. They suffer from the misconception that more is better. They'll say "sixteen to sixty"—a range that covers at least three separate audiences. Or they'll define their market as "every mom in America." But the secret of most successful start-ups is the ability to hit a bull's-eye—to aim with exquisite specificity. For example, we looked at KanDi Swim, a very cute line of bikinis inspired by desserts. Cupcakes, ice cream sundaes, rainbow cookies—you get the picture. The concept was sweet—and that means young. We encouraged them to rethink their market concept to focus on teens.

When you're doing market research, don't forget to consider ways your product can piggyback on others. For example, an unexplored market for the wedding runner we discussed above is the industry of wedding planners who make decisions about everything for the big day. Or your product might enhance something that already exists.

THE BIG IDEA TOOLBOX
GET-IT-RIGHT RESOURCES

WEB DOMAIN NAMES
* GoDaddy.com (www.godaddy.com): The world's largest domain name registrar.
* Network Solutions (www.networksolutions.com): Domain names and registration information.
* Register.com (www.register.com): Domain registration site.

PERFECT PACKAGING
* *Package Design* magazine (www.packagedesignmag.com): News and information for professional package designers.

✳ TheDieline.com (thedieline.com): The leading package design blog.

PRICING SAVVY

✳ *The Strategy and Tactics of Pricing: A Guide to Growing More Profitably*, by Thomas T. Nagle and John Hogan.
✳ *The Price Advantage*, by Michael V. Marn, Eric V. Roegner, and Craig C. Zawada.

GENERAL INFORMATION AND SUPPORT

✳ Idea Tango (www.ideatango.com): A resource Web site for inventors and businesses.
✳ *Brandweek* (www.brandweek.com): The source for branding news and advice.

DONNY'S DO: FOCUS, FOCUS, FOCUS

The number one obstacle businesses face when they're ready to grow is the temptation to spread themselves too thin and lose their focus. You have to keep holding the mirror up to your company and asking the key questions: What do you want to be known for? Who are you serving?

Stay true to yourself and your purpose.

The mission statement comes first. Before you make a single call, you have to define and internalize what you're all about. That means answering these three questions: Why are you doing it? What are you doing? How will you do it? The why, what, and how of your mission statement will set the course for everything you do.

CHAPTER 7

Break Out of the Box

I am drawn to people who choose to zig when the world zags. It is the ultimate form of freedom, and in that place of freedom, greatness happens. If you're locked into convention, if you're constantly measuring yourself against rules someone else has imposed, you've put a ceiling on what's possible. The most successful people in the world are those who separate themselves from the pack and dare to be different.

This lesson was hammered home to me at Deutsch. Every time we scored, it was on the heels of innovation. It always amazed me when a client would hire us to build their businesses, then balk at a new approach and say, "But we've always done it *this* way." By the same token, agencies can get complacent over time and stop fighting to maintain an edge.

Trust me, there are as many deadheads in the ad world as there are in other industries. A few years back, I gave a speech at a conference of the Association of National Advertisers that made a sensation. I've never won any popularity contests among my agency peers, but this time I really pissed some people off. I told them that any agency afraid to have its clients challenge longstanding business practices deserved to go under. Forget about loyalty. So what if the agency did a fabulous job forty years ago. Were they *still* doing a fabulous job? If a client didn't believe their work was the best in its category, they should fire their agency and give the business to a shop that would give them the best. And it didn't matter how many awards their agency won.

It is not a successful formula to keep doing things the same way because it worked in the past. If you want to achieve a competitive edge, you'll focus on creating something that will strike a nerve *tomorrow*. That message is more important than ever because the world you're communicating to is changing rapidly. The boxes are exploding all around us. Ten years ago, there was no widespread Internet accessibility and there was no mobile technology. The universe was confined. Today, there are no limits, and the winners are going to be the businesses that step courageously into that open arena.

If you're just starting out, being different is your *only* edge. You can't compete on experience or size. Unless you can strike a fresh nerve, you can't win. I'll take it a step further. I don't care what you're doing, if you can't honestly say that you're bringing something new and different to the marketplace—something that adds value—what's the point?

The Five Qualities of an Innovator

There's a story about a guy named Charles H. Duell, who was the director of the U.S. Patent Office in 1899. He is said to have made this statement: "Everything that can be invented has been invented." Whoa! *Time to close up shop, Charlie. Maybe you could retire and spend your evenings watching television . . . or hop in your car and drive over to the mall to catch a flick!*

I don't know if this is a true story, but it makes the point about a mentality that is *still* rampant in business and industry today, in spite of the clear evidence that success and innovation go hand in hand. Don't lend any of those people your Black-Berry or your iPhone.

So, what does it really mean to be an innovator? What are the qualities of the businesses and individuals that break out of the box? I'll give you five.

• Quality 1: Innovators ask, "How would I approach this business challenge if I had no preconceived notions of how it should be done?"
At the agency, when my creative people started developing a concept, I always told them, "Start with a blank page." Warmed-over ideas just weren't acceptable.

I'll give you an example. Let's say you've decided to start a modeling agency and you're laying out your game plan. What's the first step? Find the models that will create your signature style. Everyone knows the qualities of good models, right? They're tall, they're thin, they're beautiful, they have chiseled features, they have luxurious hair. But wait! What if you didn't already have those assumptions? What if the ideal model was short, stocky, and, dare I say, *ugly*? That was the completely upside-down view that launched Ugly Talent NY. It takes some balls to call anyone ugly, but this daring agency recognized the need for models who were not traditionally beautiful—who were real, interesting, unique characters. Simon Rogers, the creator, finds his models everywhere—on the subways, on the street—and these true originals make thousands of dollars a day. Suddenly, the world of modeling has been opened up. *Anyone* can be a model.

Big Idea Lesson: **Check your preconceptions at the door.**

• Quality 2: Innovators don't care that it's never been done. In fact, they love it. "It's never been done" has got to rank up

there as the stupidest reason not to pursue a new idea. It leaves no room for change.

Here are two sisters who *literally* broke out of the box and did what had never been done because they opened their eyes to the possibility of the U.S. mail. We brought Melissa and Michele Sipolt on the show because we were blown away by the uniqueness of their business, SENDaBALL. Melissa, a direct marketing professional, knew that you could mail just about anything if you could put a stamp on it. She was looking for an original way to celebrate a friend's new baby, so she went to the drugstore and bought a big vinyl ball. With a Sharpie pen, she wrote, "Have a ball with your new baby" on one side and the name and address of the recipient on the opposite side—and then she mailed it. That first gift started a *snowball* effect, which is something that happens when an idea is truly original and appealing. Every ball the SENDaBALL Sisters sent led to new orders. Friends started asking them to send balls to clients and friends, and before they knew it they were showing up at the post office with bags of balls. You'd think the post office would be annoyed, but as Melissa so accurately observed, "Revenue is revenue."

Big Idea Lesson: The only reason it's never been done is because nobody decided to do it—not because it can't be done.

They started the business in the garage, doing each ball by hand, and before they knew it they were shipping one hundred balls a day, charging their clients ten dollars a ball.

At the point we brought them on *The Big Idea*, they were just starting to take off. I was sure this was a million-dollar idea. Think of how many people send flowers and food baskets by mail. By taking the greeting and gift concept out of the box, they were on a roll. What struck me about this idea was the number of people who said, "I didn't know you could send a ball through the mail." Exactly! It had never been done.

• Quality 3: Innovators don't believe it has *already* been done. In virtually every category there is room for innovation—a unique twist on an existing concept.

Anshuman Vohra told us how he and his partner, David Kanbar, encountered an endgame mindset repeatedly when they tried to find a distributor for Bulldog Gin. They were convinced that there was a place in the market for a gin with sex appeal—both in the flavor and in the packaging. Their bottle design was definitely outside the norm. Instead of the typical stuffy gin image, they blew it out with a dark, stout bottle with a spiked collar around the neck. Their aim was to appeal to a younger audience with a product that was "not your grandpa's gin." So what did they hear from distributors? One after the other told Anshuman and David, "You're crazy coming out with a new gin. Nobody drinks gin anymore." They were also told that the current gin producers were doing the job just fine. No need for interlopers.

> **Big Idea Lesson: When the conglomerates turn you down, find companies that are hungry and willing to take the risk. They'll make the best partners.**

One day, after yet another refusal, Anshuman went home and started thinking. That's when he had an important realization. "I saw it clearly," he said. "We viewed the world differently. I was looking at going forward. They were looking at the past." That insight motivated him to keep pressing forward, this time choosing smaller distributors, one of which said yes.

David hit the nail on the head when he observed, "Greatness doesn't come from being able to analyze the past. Greatness comes from being able to predict the future."

• Quality 4: Innovators are champions of individuality.

You can't be an innovator if you believe that one size fits all. That was certainly true for Shoshanna Lonstein Gruss. As a teenager, Shoshanna was bustier than the average girl. And while I'd be the first to say that isn't necessarily such a terrible thing, for Shoshanna it was a daily frustration. As she was otherwise tiny, she had a hell of a time finding clothes that fit. And being uncomfortable and awkward, she tended to wear baggy clothes, and that was damaging to her self-esteem. Why couldn't someone design clothes that were more inclusive of the many shapes and sizes of women's bodies?

After college, Shoshanna considered becoming a Wall Street analyst, which was the direction most of her friends were headed in. But she could feel that it wasn't right for her. Meanwhile, every time she thought about becoming a clothing designer—something she had no experience doing—her heart would start beating faster.

Big Idea Lesson: In every industry, there's a convention waiting to be defied.

She tentatively broached the subject with her dad, and he wasn't that enthusiastic. He told her, "You don't even know what you don't know." Shoshanna took it as a challenge. She moved back in with her parents, got an internship with a fashion design company, and began the process of getting educated. Starting with no capital, Shoshanna began making samples of clothing for women whose upper and lower bodies weren't a perfect match. She found a showroom that was also just starting out, and gave it a percentage to display her clothing line.

Shoshanna told me, "I hit a million walls, and I'd just turn and go down a different hallway." But in the scheme of things, Shoshanna's clothing line took off pretty quickly. The world was full of women who didn't fit the norm. Last year, the Shoshanna Collection had twenty million dollars in sales.

• **Quality 5: Innovators are disruptive. Innovators will challenge everyday assumptions.**

They're like the little kid who asks *Why* a hundred times a day. Inherently, that means people will try to shut them up and shut them down. But I believe that this willingness to disrupt the status quo is essential to a new innovation—maybe even more important than the innovation itself.

During the nineties, I got a reputation as the "bad boy" of advertising. I wasn't *really* bad. How bad could I be and still run a multimillion-dollar company? What I did was create a brand that told the world they were going to see something they'd never seen before. Our commercials weren't going to feel like commercials. We were going to push the envelope, make waves, be daring. It worked brilliantly. The industry insiders may have jeered, but our clients couldn't wait to see what we'd do next.

BIG IDEA TOOLBOX
RESOURCES FOR INVENTORS

* U.S. Patent and Trademark Office (www.uspto.gov): The first stop for patent, trademark, and copyright information.
* General search for patents (www.google.com/patents).
* *Inventors Digest* (www.inventorsdigest.com): The Invention Magazine for Idea People.
* The Inventors Assistance Center (1-800-786-9199): Basic information on filling out patent applications.
* Enventys (www.enventys.com): Integrated solutions for product development.
* *Everyday Edisons* (www.everydayedisons.com): *Everyday Edisons*, a PBS television show, introduces viewers to the process of invention and helps them understand how to take their own ideas to the next level.
* INPEX (www.inpex.com): The largest trade show for inventors.

(continued)

* QVC (www.qvcproductsearch.com): Find out how you can present your idea to QVC or participate in one of its product search events.

DONNY'S DO: HOME-GROWN INNOVATION

We can all be innovators. Look around your house—in the kitchen, in the living room, in the bedroom. There are million-dollar ideas just waiting to be discovered. Every day, ordinary people just like you literally find millions in plain sight in their homes. All you have to do is open your closets and cupboards and start asking questions.

CHAPTER 8

Change the World with a Simple Idea

John and Bert Jacobs embody everything *The Big Idea* is about. They had a simple concept, launched it on the street for a couple hundred dollars, and literally changed the way millions of people think about their day. Three little words—*Life is Good*—have become a wearable motto for men, women, children, and even dogs. The feel-good line has not only become iconic, but it has allowed the Jacobs brothers to do good, too, through a thriving charitable arm.

When you meet John Jacobs, you'd never guess that he sits atop an eighty-million-dollar company. He's low-key and delightful, living the good life in the happiest way possible. The story of how he and his brother Bert started the Life is Good line is the kind of story we love to hear on *The Big Idea*, because not a single aspiring entrepreneur could hear it and not think, "That could be me."

In 1989, John and Bert started designing and selling T-shirts at street fairs and on college campuses, sometimes traveling for weeks at a time to eke out a meager living. Their home base was a self-described "dive," where they drew their concepts on the walls.

The big idea came after they'd been selling T-shirts for six years. They'd just returned from a lackluster road trip, and decided to throw a keg party for their friends. Over beer, they asked people to critique their wall drawings and add their comments. This home-brewed focus group yielded pure gold.

The morning after the party, John was staring at the wall, and he noticed that most of the comments were centered around a smiley-faced guy sketched by Bert. Huh, he thought, something about that smiley-faced guy is resonating. One friend wrote, "This guy's got life figured out."

On a hunch, John and Bert spent all but seventy-eight dollars of their funds to print forty-eight T-shirts, featuring the smiley-faced guy and the inscription "Life is Good." They took them to a street fair in Cambridge, along with some of their other shirts. Within forty-five minutes of opening, all forty-eight shirts were sold. They were shocked, not just by the sales, but by the diversity of the buyers, which included a tattooed Harley rider, a schoolteacher, and a kid. Could it be that they'd found the universal message?

"It scared the hell out of us," John admitted. "We had been searching for a message, an icon, for years, and this was it. We knew it."

They kept printing the shirts, gave the smiley-faced guy an identity as Jake, and slowly began getting orders from boutiques in the area. They did eighty-two thousand dollars in business the first year, doubled it the second year, and tripled it the third year. They kept their ears to the ground and responded to their customers by adding other whimsical drawings—Jake on a bike, Jake swimming—as well as new items. Today the Life is Good brand is on everything from hats to soccer balls to dog dishes to coffee mugs.

The Jacobs brothers had found success, and that's when they made the transition to something much bigger. Life is Good received many memorable and moving letters over the years from people who felt a special bond with their products and the simple, optimistic messages they carried. This was especially true of people who faced great adversity. Providing hope and relief in a time of adversity was the motivation for Life is Good's first significant fund-raising effort. After 9/11, John and Bert were struck by how many people were suddenly asking, "*Is* life good?" They decided to do a fund-raiser for the families of victims. Their American flag T-shirt raised $207,000 for United Way.

After that experience, John and Bert realized they had a mission that transcended T-shirts, caps, and coffee mugs. They saw an opportunity to have a sustained, positive impact through charitable giving, and good, old-fashioned outdoor festivals seemed just right for their brand and their values.

Since 2003, Life is Good has held numerous blowout festivals, including a Pumpkin Festival in Boston attended by 100,000 people, which raised $600,000, and a Life is Good Festival at Fenway Park that raised $800,000. They established the Life is Good Kids Foundation to distribute all money raised

> **Big Idea Lesson: In an age where negativity is a best-selling brand, Life is Good broke out of the pack and delivered a message of hope.**

nationally through Life is Good Festivals to the best organizations serving children facing unfair challenges.

I really believe that the reason John and Bert's company has been so successful is that they understood that their clever idea was more than just an empty slogan. They're selling tangible forms of possibility.

Do-Gooder Nation

I want to take a minute to applaud the many entrepreneurs whose vision of the American dream transcends personal wealth. So many of these people started their businesses on a wing and a prayer, and when they succeeded, the first thing they did was ask, "How can I make someone else's dream come true?"

The idea of doing well by doing good is not exactly new, but in the last decade it has definitely caught on. The qualities that make someone a great entrepreneur—passion, vision, persistence—are exactly what's needed for those who aim to change the world.

BIG IDEA TOOLBOX
RESOURCES FOR SOCIAL ENTREPRENEURS

* The Institute for Social Entrepreneurs (www.socialent.org): Provides seminars, workshops, and consulting services for social entrepreneurs in the United States and around the world.
* Commongood Careers (www.commongoodcareers.org): A nonprofit job search firm that is dedicated to helping today's most effective social entrepreneurs hire the best talent.
* Idealist.org (www.idealist.org): A global clearinghouse of nonprofit and volunteer resources.
* GreenBiz.com (www.greenbiz.com): News on green businesses and sustainable business practices.
* Green Dreams (www.greendreams.com): A guide to green business practices.
* Greenopia (www.greenopia.com): A guide to doing everything you do—greener.
* *How to Change the World: Social Entrepreneurs and the Power of New Ideas*, by David Bornstein. A blueprint for progressive companies.

A Company With *Sole*

Most people know Blake Mycoskie as a popular contestant on the reality television show *The Amazing Race*. I got to know Blake as the creator of a phenomenal big idea that is changing the world, one pair of shoes at a time. And it started with an investment of only five hundred dollars.

Blake's company, TOMS Shoes, was born out of a trip to Argentina, where Blake witnessed impoverished children walking the streets without footwear. Blake asked himself, what if he could provide shoes for these kids? He came up with the idea of TOMS Shoes, designing a shoe based on the lightweight Argentinean shoe called *alpargatas*, and the promise that for every shoe sold in America, he'd send one pair of shoes to Argentina.

In 2006, TOMS organized their first official "shoe drop" in Argentina, after his company reached the goal of selling 10,000 shoes. Blake and his staff personally delivered the shoes, which was a big high for them. In 2007, the company made its second shoe drop of 50,000 shoes to South African children living in poverty.

Big Idea Lesson: People like to make a contribution. If you can feed a piece of your customer's soul while providing a product or service, you'll have a winning sales pitch.

The charitable cause behind the business is probably a big factor that draws potential customers to purchase TOMS shoes. Blake is a perfect example of how it doesn't take much money to make a big difference—and some big bucks!

DONNY'S DO: TAKE ON THE WORLD

As the world grows smaller, the opportunities for people of vision to make a difference grow bigger. You can take on the world in your own backyard, and many entrepreneurs are doing just that. Here's an example. Increasingly, the people coming on our show are producing environmentally friendly products. It has almost become second nature. Yet environmental consciousness is relatively new—unfortunately. Overnight, consumers have started demanding a cleaner, safer, more organic world—and the smart businesses are those who got a head start. The visionaries making big bucks are the do-gooders who got there first.

No Is Not an Option

CHAPTER 9

Why NOT Me?

W hen you say "Why NOT me?" it's a spiritual declaration that informs everything else you'll ever do. You can't make it until you believe it. The most successful people in the world have an almost naïve sense of entitlement. They don't tell you, "I'm going to try and write a novel." They tell you, "I'm going to write the next great American novel."

"Why NOT me?" transforms your worldview and exponentially broadens your arena. I'll give you an example. A few years ago, I voiced a dream of mine out loud. I said I'd like to be mayor of New York. Where did I get off making such a preposterous statement? Well, why NOT me? Mike Bloomberg, the current mayor, was a businessman who beat out all the conventional politicians. The idea wasn't so wild.

But here's the interesting part. Suddenly, people were asking, "Is Donny Deutsch going to run for mayor?" Every article that was written about me after that point mentioned that I might run for mayor. Now, the day before I said it, no one ever looked at me and thought, "He's mayoral material." No one even put my name in the same sentence with the word *mayor*. But once it was out there, suddenly the door was open a crack. It was a possibility I was free to pursue. I still get asked if I'm going to run for mayor. Who knows? I might someday.

I meet so many people who are afraid to voice their dreams and desires. They think if they edge that door open even a little, it will slam shut in their faces. But it's not just the fear of getting laughed out of the room. This obsequiousness is bred into us. How many of us were taught from childhood to be humble—don't be cocky, don't be brash, don't be boastful, don't forget that pride goeth before a fall? That mentality creates followers, not leaders. No one ever became successful by saying "NOT me."

"You're never more alive than when you're on the cusp of madness." That was Alton Brown, the unlikely star of two food shows, on *The Big Idea,* describing his decision to completely chuck his old life and enter the culinary world in his mid-thirties. I love that quality—call it confidence or call it insanity—that gives certain people a rush when they're climbing a mountain without a safety rope. When Alton said, "Why shouldn't I have a cooking show—I could do it better," he wasn't even in the food business. So he took the bold step of going to culinary school, shooting his own TV pilots, and pitching them to the Food Network. Alton's courage came from the deep certainty that he could succeed—and the understanding that he would be okay if he didn't.

The point is, until you say "Why NOT me?" the door is closed on every dream. And the earlier in life you figure that out, the better off you are. Most of us don't get it until we've already been beaten down a bit. That's why I was so taken with Miley Cyrus. If you have kids, you know who Miley is. In her television persona of Hannah Montana, she's the idol of seventeen million kids, ages two to eleven. Miley is a billion-dollar brand at the ripe old age of sixteen. I had her on *The Big Idea* because of what she managed to pull off at the age of eleven. That's when she auditioned for Hannah Montana, even though she was completely wrong for the part. For one thing, she was four years too young—the part called for a fifteen-year-old. For another thing, she had practically no acting experience. The folks at Disney politely told her she wasn't what they were looking for. But Miley wouldn't take no for an answer. She really wanted that part. I got such a kick out of her drive. She said, "I thought, maybe if I keep bugging them, they'll give in." Remember, she was *eleven* at the time. How did she finally turn Disney around? She said, "I begged and begged, for a whole year, and finally they had to say yes."

Beg and beg until you get what you want? What kind of a screwball business plan is *that*? All I can say is that out of the mouths of babes sometimes come great pearls of wisdom.

The Entitlement Exercise

What are you entitled to in your life? Make a list. Write it down:

I'm entitled to . . . do work I love.

I'm entitled to . . . run my own life.

I'm entitled to . . . live without worrying about the bills.

I'm entitled to . . . be married to the love of my life.

I'm entitled to . . . raise my family in a positive environment.

I'm entitled to . . . lead the team.

I'm entitled to . . . own a great house, or even two houses.

I'm entitled to . . . be the head of my department.

I'm entitled to . . . get that loan.

I'm entitled to . . . sit in the box seats.

I'm entitled to . . . be president of the United States.

Once you've got your list, *own* it. Make it your mantra. But don't stop there. The power of positive thinking isn't enough, if you don't use the power of positive *doing*. Gary Coxe, a personal growth expert and life strategist, who has come on *The*

Big Idea to offer advice to budding entrepreneurs, has a great line. He says, "Positive thinking is like spray paint on rust. It doesn't last long." In other words, saying "Why NOT me?" is the door-opener. To get things in motion, you have to walk through the door.

Take an item on your entitlement list. What are the practical actions you need to take to get moving? For the fun of it, let's try a non-business example. You feel entitled to be married to the love of your life. How is that going to happen? A few years ago, the *Today* show invited me to participate in a series hosted by Ann Curry on the subject of finding a mate. When they first called, I was surprised, to say the least. They wanted *me* to advise women about dating? I thought they'd speed-dialed the wrong number. I don't exactly have a glowing track record in that department. But then it was explained to me that the title of the segment was "How to Be the CEO of Your Love Life." This was about using real-life business principles to find love. "Okay," I told them, "I can do that." It fascinated me that the same people who create brilliant business plans and market the hell out of their companies are paralyzed when it comes to their personal lives. You wouldn't start a company and just sit back and wait for customers to find you. Why do that with dating?

The show was fun—and instructive. My subject was a lovely divorced woman, accomplished in business, but stuck when it came to finding love. She didn't know how to make a move. She was brave enough to go on national television to learn how to apply business principles to love. We went through the steps—just as you would if you were launching a company:

1. What is your mission statement? (Do you want to date casually, do you want to be married in a year, do you want to begin a serious relationship in six months?)

2. What is your profile? (What is unique, fascinating, appealing about you?)

3. Who's the target market? (Are you looking for a young professional, a mature man, a religious person, a fitness nut?)

4. What's your media plan? (Where are you going to advertise
yourself? Are you going to join a group, hit the dog walk, take a
seminar?)

5. Who's on your board of directors? (Name the friends that are
going to help you get your plan in motion.)

By the time we were finished, she was a different person—at
least, that's what her friends said. Even I could see it. She was
energized by the prospect of putting herself out there. She had
confidence. If you think about it, every issue in life can be re-
solved with this simple two-step: dream plus action.

Success Is a Democracy

No one ever accused me of being a genius. Just ask my fourth-
grade teacher. I'm a smart guy. I have some God-given talents.
But I'm no genius. I've made my share of boners, and I know I'll
make more.

Some people look at very successful individuals and say, "Oh,
this guy made a hundred million dollars . . . I could never do
that." Or, "This woman built a business empire . . . I could
never do that." They think they're looking at people of excep-
tional brilliance. It's true, there are occasional geniuses that
come along, people like Bill Gates. But it's not the norm. I've
met thousands of successful people in my life, and most of them
are not geniuses. They're tenacious bulldogs with a sense of entitlement that spurs them ahead. They get an idea and run with
it because they believe they can. I've spent many years in rooms
with CEOs, and often I left scratching my head, thinking, "How
did *that* guy get there?" But if their genius wasn't self-evident,
their drive was.

My goal on *The Big Idea* is to democratize success. It's not for someone else. When you realize that you deserve it, too, it's demystified and reachable. That's the principle of democracy: bottom-up, not top-down.

Now, you've got to know that when you take on the establishment, there will be some circling of wagons. Look at Tim Walsh, who decided to break into the toy industry with a board game. That's tough. The forty-billion-dollar toy industry is practically impossible to crack from the outside, because all the big companies have their own development teams. But Tim persisted because he was confident that he had the next great game.

Tim and his friends Dave Yearick and Ed Muccini invented TriBond while they were students at Colgate University. Their goal was to create a game that presented an intellectual challenge, but with a broader appeal than Trivial Pursuit. This is the basic concept: TriBond asks, "What do these three things have in common?" Players try to guess the common bond between three clues. For example, what is the common bond between Florida, a locksmith, and a piano? They have keys.

It took Tim and his friends two years to get a prototype together, and then off they went to sell it to a toy manufacturer. That's where they hit a brick wall. Milton Bradley, Parker Brothers, Mattel, and Tyco all turned them down flat.

If the big boys say no, where do you go? This is another lesson I've heard time and again—you go to the *little* guys. Tim joined forces with a small manufacturer, Patch Products, which produced the game and hired Tim to market it. The first thing he did was contact radio DJs throughout the country. He asked them to play TriBond with their listeners in return for games to give away. It proved to be one of their most successful promotions. Within three years, they'd sold over one million copies of the game.

The best revenge? The day Mattel came to Tim looking for a licensing deal. That was a sweet victory. Today, TriBond is a Mattel best seller.

Where do you get the confidence to crack the toy mafia? First, you *believe* you've got a winner. Second, you realize you've got history on your side. So many great games or hit toys were created in someone's basement or at the kitchen table by people who had no connection with the industry. Monopoly was invented by a down-and-out salesman during the Depression. Trivial Pursuit was the brainstorm of a couple of guys who were bored with Scrabble. Cabbage Patch Kids were created by an art student. Who says you have to be a card-carrying member of the toy industry to succeed? Tim Walsh turned his sense of entitlement into millions.

Big Idea Lesson: Success is a democracy. Don't let anyone tell you that you can't join.

THE AMERICAN DREAM SELF-SABOTAGE TEST

Are you standing in the way of your own success? Take this test to find out.

1. Do you ever ask, "Why should I try to be successful?" ☐ Yes ☐ No

2. Do you consider money dirty, un-cool, or pretentious? ☐ Yes ☐ No

3. Do you have a negative opinion about wealthy people? ☐ Yes ☐ No

4. Are you afraid of making more money than your parents? ☐ Yes ☐ No

5. When you walk into a room, do you prefer to remain unnoticed? ☐ Yes ☐ No

6. Do you tend to refuse opportunities
   to give to charity? ☐ Yes ☐ No

7. When you lose money on a bad deal,
   do you hold on to regret? ☐ Yes ☐ No

How many *yes* answers did you give? These are indications that you may be sabotaging your business success. Remember, money isn't a bad thing. The more money you make, the more good you can do for yourself and others.

Bypass the Pecking Order

When Tyler Dikman came on *The Big Idea* he was only twenty-three, but here's the kicker. Tyler had already been in business for eight years. He started his tech consulting company, CoolTronics, in high school, and he graduated with over a million dollars in the bank. Tyler's story is striking because conventional society has a bias against really young people rising to the top. This mentality is ingrained into our culture—you have to earn your stripes, start in the mailroom and crawl up the ladder rung by rung. Steve Jobs likes to tell the story of how he and Steve Wozniak took their personal computer invention to Hewlett-Packard, and they weren't interested. They said, "You haven't even finished college yet." These young geniuses weren't rejected on the merits of their idea. They were rejected because some bonehead thought they were too young to be so successful. They hadn't *suffered* enough!

That's the thing about technology, though. It's *owned* by the young. Who do you call if something goes wrong with your computer? Chances are, it's the high school student down the street. Tyler knew how to fix computers, and he talked his parents into letting him run a business out of their home. His motto was: "We are the concierge of your computer." He hired his high school friends to work for him, and he paid them more than they'd make at a fast food restaurant or the local car wash. They were never at a loss for clients. By the time he was seventeen, Tyler was hobnobbing with the likes of Bill Gates and Michael Dell.

When you meet Tyler, you don't see an arrogant guy who thinks he's better than everyone else. You see a young

> **Big Idea Lesson:** If you've got a revolutionary idea, expect the chorus to clamor against you—and then do it anyway. Someday the naysayers will be working for *you*.

man with pure passion for his work, and, yes, a youthful enthusiasm for what's still possible. Tyler knows how to use his youth to win over support, and he has advice for other young entrepreneurs. "Be the kid they wish they had." He's pretty smart for a twenty-three-year-old.

WHO . . . ME?

Anyone who thinks he or she can't possibly rise to the top or pursue a distant dream should take a page from Sarah Reinertsen's book. Sarah, who is missing a leg, remembers being envious and frustrated in high school when she wasn't picked for the kickball team or asked to dance. She was barraged with messages about all the things a kid with a prosthetic leg *couldn't* do. But she got the best revenge by training as an athlete and becoming the first female leg amputee to complete the Iron Man Triathlon World Championship in Hawaii. After Sarah appeared on *The Big Idea*, she had a wonderful insight that I want to share with you. Sarah said, "I may have been the only amputee on today's show, but I wasn't the only one with a disability. I actually believe that almost all of us have a 'disability' of some sort; some are just less obvious than others. While my disability is physical, a couple of the guests on the show admitted to having hidden disabilities like dyslexia, or just tough circumstances in their childhood. Each of us overcame our obstacles, hidden or obvious, to forge our own paths to success."

CHAPTER 10

The Gut Check
Moment

I n every endeavor, there's going to be at least one moment—and sometimes several—when you clinch and say, "I can't do this. The boulder is too big to push up the hill."

That's the gut check moment. It's the ultimate test of how much you want it, how much you believe in it, and how much you're willing to put up with to achieve it.

I'm not talking about the little bumps in the road that every business encounters. I'm talking about events that clearly could be deal breakers. A personal tragedy derails a career. A first shipment arrives and the product is spoiled. A factory burns down. A major client bails with fifty percent of your business. It's do-or-die time.

I always think of the scene in the movie *Wall Street*, when Bud Fox, the Charlie Sheen character, says, "Man looks in the abyss, there's nothing staring back at him. At that moment, man finds his character. And that is what keeps him out of the abyss." I know. It sounds melodramatic. But if you've ever had the abyss open up, you'll recognize the truth of those words.

Maureen Kelly, the creator of Tarte Cosmetics, who is frequently on the show, had the ultimate gut check moment: 9/11. Maureen is a real dynamo; there's no doubt she could achieve anything she put her mind to. With the emotional and financial support of her husband, Mark, she got her innovative cosmetics line off the ground. The chic, luxurious, and fun cosmetics earned her a spot at Henri Bendel, and she was on her way.

Maureen's husband always encouraged her, telling her, "Life is too short not to follow your dream." In his case, life was tragically short. Mark, a bond trader with Keefe, Bruyette & Woods, was on the eighty-ninth floor of the South Tower of the World Trade Center on 9/11, and he died in the attack. That was Maureen's gut check moment. In the aftermath of such an unthinkable catastrophe, most of Maureen's friends and family expected her to throw in the towel on her business. Maureen refused to consider it. If anything, Mark's death made her more determined to honor his memory by living fully and pursuing the dream he helped her believe in. Tarte Cosmetics has grown phenomenally in the last six years. Maureen has a wonderful life spirit and a natural business sense. I've been so impressed with her that I've often brought her on *The Big Idea* to give advice to entrepreneurs who are pitching new products.

Many of the successful people who come on the show are fearless about their gut check moments because in early childhood they faced enormous obstacles. They weren't the prom queens or football stars that peaked in the eleventh grade. They had to fight for it—and that toughened them.

I have been most inspired by the people who were dealt a lousy hand, but they took what they were dealt and transcended it. It puts things into perspective for those of us who had supportive parents and relatively crisis-free childhoods. Their stories never stop being inspirational.

If you watch the Food Network, you're probably familiar with Sandra Lee, creator of Semi-Homemade Cooking. Sandra is gorgeous, bright, innovative, and a natural television personality. But when I had Sandra on *The Big Idea*, I told her straight out, "If I had met you at age fifteen, you're the last person I would have expected to be sitting here."

Sandra's life story is a heartbreaker. She was born to a teen-age mother who was totally incapable of taking care of her and her sister. When Sandra was two, her mother dropped them off at her grandmother's, said she was going out for milk, and didn't come back for four years. For the next five years, Sandra and her siblings—now four of them—endured poverty and abuse, until their mother died. At age ten, Sandra became a surrogate mother for her brothers and sisters, and basically raised them on her own. Incidentally, that's when she got interested in cooking as she tried to be creative with welfare and food stamps. She told me, "I was the queen of Bisquick."

When she was fifteen, Sandra went to live with her stepfather in another state. Within a year, he was in prison on an assault charge, and she was on her own. While still in high school, Sandra was forced to rent her own apartment and get a job to support herself.

Sandra was driven to make something of her life, but how did she push herself to overcome such awesome barriers? Where did she get the motivation to succeed when her only role models had been failure? For Sandra, it was simple. "I wasn't going to turn out like them," she said. "I wanted to be a different person. The strength came from within. It's deciding you will be the person you want to be."

Big Idea Lesson: If you want to succeed in life, write your own script. Don't be shackled to the failed scripts of the past.

The Comeback Kids

What separates the winners from the losers is not whether or not they've had a catastrophe. It's what they did next. How many times have you seen a famous person who was knocked down by a crushing blow, and you thought, "Well, that's the end of the road"? Most of us look at these train wrecks in life and business, and we can't imagine how there could be a comeback.

Martha Stewart is a perfect example. I admire Martha. I think she's a great lady. I've interviewed her on *The Big Idea*. She even had me on her show and tried—not very successfully— to teach me how to cook. Martha was a businesswoman who always seemed to be in perfect control of her message and her life. Then she landed in jail on an insider trading charge. Being sent to jail has got to rank up there as about the worst calamity that could befall a person of Martha's level of achievement. Most people would have been crippled by the shame, not to mention the financial hit the businesses took. During her five months in prison, Martha's multimedia conglomerate was rocked. Share prices that had once been above forty-nine dollars tumbled to slightly more than five dollars. Her television show was canceled and advertisers abandoned her magazine.

Martha did two things that were very courageous. First, she embraced her prison experience and spent her time mentoring the other inmates, leading the press to dub the prison "Camp Cupcake." Her second act of courage occurred after she left prison. She didn't seclude herself. She didn't wallow in self-pity. Without fanfare, she returned to work and threw herself into bringing her business back. Instead of becoming a symbol of corporate shame, Martha has become a symbol of personal strength.

Donald Trump is another one. Trump has a reputation for being arrogant and ruthless, but I know him personally, and what impresses me most is that this is a guy who loves being in the game. He refuses to be defeated. Trump is so successful that many people don't realize that his rise has included a number of dramatic setbacks—notably his near-bankruptcy in the early

1990s. His comeback from the brink was a testament to his audacity and his business genius.

I have a regular celebrity segment on the show, but my focus is different from the typical fawning approach you see in the entertainment media. When I interview celebrities, I'm not interested in hearing a catalog of their greatest hits. I want to know about the hard times, because that's where you find the kernel of wisdom. If you put celebrities on a pedestal, and give them an aura of invincibility, it takes them out of the game. There's nothing to learn. I believe that the value to viewers is to hear how these successful individuals overcame the worst challenges of their lives.

Many viewers told us how moved they were by the interview I did with Sean Combs—known as Diddy (he dropped the *P*). He agreed to come on the show because he wanted to let kids know that the hip-hop world isn't an instant road to riches. He wasn't an overnight success, and there were no shortcuts in his career. He got there through years of long hours and hard work—and a lifetime of gut check moments.

Sean Combs had two strikes against him from the start. His father, an associate of a leading drug lord, was murdered in Central Park when Sean was three. His mother worked several jobs just to keep food on the table, and he credits her with instilling the discipline and values that kept him from following in his father's footsteps. Sean's early grit was on full display when he established himself at age thirteen as the "most successful paperboy in history." He had routes all over the area, and at one point was pulling in six hundred dollars a week. But his true love was music. In college, all his friends were getting internships at law offices and financial firms. He begged Andre Harrell, the head of Uptown Records, to take him on as an unpaid intern, and he soaked up every lesson he could, working two years without pay. He told me, "It was never about the money. It was about the music. I'd have worked ten years for free if I'd had to."

His first big gut check moment came at age twenty-two when

he was just hitting his stride at Uptown Records and he got fired. Diddy has examined those years, and he's brutally honest about his failures. "I got too big for my britches," he told me. "I started getting caught up with success. I was running around the castle with a crown, but the castle already had a king, and I was naked." Diddy admits that he'd gone off track, lost respect for the people above him, stopped being a team player. He didn't even see it coming. But one day Andre walked into his office and told him he was out. He also uttered those comfortless words: "This is going to hurt me more than it hurts you."

Diddy was in utter shock. "I hoped I was dreaming," he said. "I cried and cried for days. I was heartbroken." But looking back, he also gets that being fired was a necessary step in his maturing process. He came back, more humble, with a clearer vision, and having more respect for the business. Teaming up with the legendary Clive Davis, he was incredibly successful.

But the gut checks didn't end there. What he calls "the worst day of my life" was still ahead of him. That was the day his best friend and the hip-hop star he'd discovered, Notorious B.I.G., was gunned down before his eyes as they were leaving an industry event. Diddy was shaken to the core. He went into a terrible depression. This wasn't just a job loss or a business failure. This was a potentially insurmountable life crisis. So what did he do? First, he tapped into what he loved, making a tribute recording to B.I.G. called "I'll Be Missing You." But in the long run, Diddy said, there is no solution to pain. You have to fight the feeling, day by day, for as long as it takes to climb out of the hole.

Big Idea Lesson: Build your inner strengths the same way you build your muscles, and draw on them during the inevitable crises of life and business.

Diddy's story was inspiring to all of us. Here's a guy who drew on tremendous internal resources to overcome tremendous obstacles.

A Life-and-Death Gut Check

What started out as a fun and passionate adventure led to a real life-and-death gut check for Heather Birdwell. Heather made quite an impression on *The Big Idea*—six feet tall, strong, blond, gorgeous—clearly a woman who liked to live on the edge. But in 2006, she nearly fell over the cliff.

A little background. When Heather and her sister Holly were kids, they spent weekends with dad riding motorcycles, ATVs, and dune buggies. Their site of choice was Glamis, a stretch of mountainous sand dunes in Southern California that attracted thousands of riders every year. Heather and Holly's shared passion for off-road motor sports led to an ingenious business concept. They were frustrated by the lack of female gear for bikers, and they resented having to buy men's clothing. And that's how Damzl, a line of women's biker gear, with the slogan "Feminize the machine," was born.

Heather and Holly knew they had a big idea, and their dad agreed. He invested in their fledgling business, and they took it on the road, selling gear out of their signature pink trailer. On one fateful weekend, they decided they were ready to sell their wares at Glamis. It was to be their big coming out.

After working all day as a vendor, Holly decided that she wanted to get a ride in before sunset. She led a pack of five ATVs, racing across the dunes. But visibility was low, and the dunes were crowded. As she was cresting a hill, Holly was struck head-on by a dune buggy, and killed.

The loss of her sister was an unimaginable tragedy for Heather. Not only was it a brutal life gut check, it was also a business gut check. Could she—*should* she—go on without Holly? As she told us on the show, "I wasn't sure whether to embrace it or crawl into a fetal position."

Unsure what to do, Heather decided that at least she had to fulfill the commitments the sisters had already made. And in the process of getting back to work, she quickly found out that throwing herself into the business was a great tool, a form of occupational therapy. She also discovered that she belonged to a community, and the support of her colleagues and friends in the field saw her through.

Big Idea Lesson: Sometimes life's greatest tragedies show us what we're really made of, testing our will and resolve. Heather passed the test, by finding the way to honor her sister and continue their shared dream.

Heather is still raw, and Damzl is still small, but growing. I have no doubt that it will become a multimillion-dollar business, because Heather has what it takes to survive the long haul.

Be Fearless

Television is one of the most cutthroat industries in the world. You're on the line every day, your face is out there, and the competitors are constantly nipping at your heels. The sword of accountability is swift and sure in the form of ratings. It's not a safe place to be, and by nature people who are attracted to television have to be fearless.

When I started at CNBC, a lot of people said, "Can this guy really make it in television? He's untested." The media was buzzing about it for a while. I had a different attitude. I chose to be fearless. Maybe I'd make it, maybe I wouldn't, but I knew I'd have been worse off for not doing it than if I tried it and failed.

The biggest lesson I've learned over the years is that you have to make failure your friend. It is amazing how many people don't get where they want to be because they're afraid of failure. Whenever I talk to super successful people, what they always want to discuss most passionately is how their biggest growth came from the lessons their failures taught them. You cannot have greatness without some failure.

Fearlessness takes many forms, and some of the most astonishing success stories happen in the midst of insurmountable odds. For example, what would you say about a business strategy like Fred DeLuca's? Each time his company looked like it was failing, he responded by opening another outlet. Who is Fred DeLuca? The founder of the ten-billion-dollar Subway chain. Fred's story is a template for fearlessness.

In 1965, Fred was just another kid from the Bronx projects trying to raise money for college. He asked a family friend what he should do, and was told, "You should open up a sandwich shop. If you're interested, I'll be your partner and give you a thousand dollars." Back then a person could actually go pretty far on a thousand bucks. Rents were cheap, and so were the ingredients Fred needed to make his sandwiches. He set up his shop, passed out flyers in the neighborhood, put his friends to work, and on the first day of operation he sold three hundred sandwiches.

Big Idea Lesson: Fred DeLuca points out that a key to Subway's survival was that his suppliers wanted him to succeed, and they kept up their support even in tough times. By making his suppliers part of the team, instead of outsiders, Fred created opportunity for all of them.

But soon sales declined because, as he says, "We didn't know what we were doing." With the threat of extinction, Fred made what he recalls as a totally oddball choice. He opened a second shop, to give the impression that they were doing well. The two stores were just getting by when he opened a third—then all three started going downhill. So he opened a fourth! And then a fifth. The fifth store finally took off, and Subway began to grow. Fred signed up the first franchisee in 1974, and today there are more than 29,000 Subway franchises around the world—including several on military bases in Iraq.

Fred DeLuca's decision to expand in hard times may seem nuts on the face of it. Few business advisers would recommend such a rocky path to growth. But Fred believed in himself and in his product, and he didn't give up until he made it work.

DONNY'S DO: EMBRACE YOUR BUTTERFLIES

The best way to prepare yourself for the unexpected upheavals that might befall you in the future is to practice everyday courage. What do I mean by that? I don't care what business you're in, there are regular moments when you're going to get butterflies. You're making a big pitch to a new client, you're delivering a report to your boss, you're giving a demonstration of your product to a buyer—fill in the blank. At that moment, even if you have all the confidence in the world, you know there's a chance you're going to get shot down. If you're not nervous as hell, you're not human. So embrace the butterflies. And when you come out the other side, remember how it felt to be fearful, and remember that you did it anyway.

CHAPTER 11

They Told Me
I'd Never Make It

Everybody knows that humans can't fly, right? If God had meant for us to fly, he would have given us wings, right? The James Bond scene in *Thunderball*, where he straps on a jetpack and escapes his captors, was just a stunt, right? An ordinary person couldn't actually *do* that, right?

Wrong, wrong, wrong, and wrong again. I know because I saw it with my own eyes. Troy Widgery, of Jet Pack International, dreamed of flying ever since he was a child and was enraptured by James Bond's feat in *Thunderball*. In 2003, Troy and two friends, John Hewatt and Dave Butler, began thinking about how they could build a personal flying machine that would be easy for the average person to actually strap on and use. Bell Aerosystems had tried it back in the 1960s, but it was a clunky model—heavy, impractical, and only operational for very short distances. Troy, John, and Dave took advantage of the most modern technological and engineering advances to create the Go Fast Jet Pack, a completely individualized flying machine. And guess what, folks? It really works.

Troy came to CNBC on a sunny spring day to demonstrate his jet pack—strapping it on to Eric Scott, his human demonstrator. We all stood on the ground and gaped as Eric shot straight up over the CNBC building and landed near the parking lot. The demonstration lasted only thirty seconds, but it seemed a lot longer. I have to say, this project thrilled me, because it touched that romantic place where all dreams can come true. Like most kids, I grew up reading the stories of early inventors, and watching films of original flying machines. It felt so last century—as if the great daring schemes were all in the past. To be an eyewitness to a twenty-first-century version of this level of innovation was a high point. James Bond had a suave, throwaway line in the movie, referring to his jet pack. He said, "No well-dressed man should be without one." Thanks to Troy Widgery, that may become a reality. Is this a great country, or what?

Which brings me to the point of this story: Never say never.

Whether it's flying machines or vegetarian chips, every successful entrepreneur I've ever met has encountered a world of doubt. It's the nature of the beast. If you've got a revolutionary idea, people are going to shoot it down, and you along with it. In fact, some of the most important ideas of the last fifty years almost never made it off the drawing table, thanks to the know-it-alls. They said it couldn't be done—and then somebody did it.

Hold the Obituary

Has anyone ever told you that your idea stinks? Cynthia Good, founder of *PINK* magazine, came on the show and told us how she got put down when she pitched her idea for a women's business magazine. Cynthia's incredibly smart, creative, and personable— she can run *my* magazine anytime. When she had the idea for *PINK*, Cynthia had already successfully produced a local business magazine for women in Atlanta, and she knew there was nothing on the national front that gave women what they really needed—advice for people like herself who wanted to be more successful in business while having more joy in their personal lives. "It's the magazine I wish I'd had when I was starting out," Cynthia told me. "Women live their lives this way. They're closing big business deals, then picking up the phone to make sure the babysitter gets milk and toilet paper. No one was addressing their needs."

Cynthia and her partner, Genevieve Bos, pitched the idea to the major women's magazine companies, like Condé Nast and Hearst. "Pretty much everybody in the industry said, 'Don't do it—you're nuts,'" Cynthia recalled. "They said, 'How are two women going to launch a magazine when we spend a hundred million dollars on a start-up?'" One expert even told them, "You can't launch a magazine. Don't you know that magazines are dead?"

What was the take-home message for Cynthia? If the world is writing your obituary and you're still breathing, don't just lie down and die. Cynthia and Genevieve started out conducting their business on a picnic table in Cynthia's backyard. They made the decision that they were going to raise advertising revenue before going to a printer. When they got a poor response from ad agencies, they went straight to the decision makers at companies, playing on the desire to support women in their own organizations. By tailoring their message to an audience that wanted to hear it, they got off the ground.

Big Idea Lesson: Listen to your own heart. If you feel a need, chances are that others feel it, too. All the denials in the world can't contradict what is real to you.

In just two years, *PINK* has an impressive readership of 450,000. It remains the only national women's business magazine—all because two women had the vision and the guts to make it happen. At the magazine, Cynthia said, they are fanatical about being a culture of possibility. "I fine employees who say *can't*."

The Best Revenge Is Making Millions

As soon as you give someone else the power to say no, you're dead in the water. Cordia Harrington, founder of the Tennessee Bun Company, is one of the most inspirational entrepreneurs to come on *The Big Idea*. Cordia's philosophy—which has made her millions—is "No is not an option."

Twenty years ago, Cordia was a struggling single mother with three small boys, who was looking for a business opportunity that would allow her to spend more time with her kids. Someone suggested she try for a McDonald's franchise, and she decided she could do it. It wasn't a simple thing. At that point, there were very few women franchise owners in the system. She had to convince the corporate bigwigs, whose first response was, "What makes you think *you* could run a McDonald's?" With sheer bravado and no experience, Cordia pushed herself to the front of the line, and when a franchise opportunity opened in Effingham, Illinois, she packed her kids in the car and went after it.

It was almost a disaster. With a mandatory payment of twenty-seven thousand dollars a month to McDonald's, Cordia needed to move a hell of a lot of hamburgers, and the customer base just wasn't there. So she decided to increase her customer base with a truly astonishing ploy. It's one of my favorite stories of all the ones I've heard on the show. Cordia took on a Greyhound bus franchise, and parked it on the corner next to her McDonald's. With eighty-eight buses a day picking up and dropping off hungry riders, her McDonald's boomed. Suddenly she was a star in the McDonald's empire.

But that wasn't enough for Cordia. After she was asked to join the McDonald's bun committee (get that—they have a *bun* committee!), she started to think about becoming a bun supplier for the chain. She was convinced she could do it better. She started asking, "How can I become a supplier?" That's when she was turned down flat—thirty-one times. In the thirty-second inter-

Big Idea Lesson: Keep knocking on doors until you find the person who will say yes to your dream. That person is out there. You just have to find him or her. Persistence *always* pays.

view, she got a yes. Today her Tennessee Bun Company grosses over fifty million dollars a year.

This is a true rags-to-riches story. No question it involved many years of struggle. Cordia worked her buns off to make her dream a reality. But the absolute key was her refusal to give up.

DO YOU HAVE MILLIONAIRE POTENTIAL? TAKE CYNTHIA GOOD'S QUIZ

Cynthia Good, CEO of *PINK* magazine, has put together a list of important questions to ask yourself in order to ensure that you have million-dollar potential. If you can dig down deep and truly answer *yes* to all the questions below, then you may just have what it takes to make millions. Remember, you need a PERFECT score.

1. Are you willing to take an honest look at your life? ☐ Yes ☐ No

2. Are you willing to say "I'm OUTTA here!"? ☐ Yes ☐ No

3. Are you willing to have doors slammed in your face? ☐ Yes ☐ No

4. Are you willing to go without sleep, and sacrifice personal time? ☐ Yes ☐ No

5. Are you willing to be different, and create something unique? ☐ Yes ☐ No

6. Are you willing to put EVERYTHING on the line? ☐ Yes ☐ No

Four Ways to Turn Around a Turndown

Even the most skillful, persistent salesperson in the world some-times has to take no for an answer. But you can make the rejec-tion work for you. What are you going to do when someone steps on your big idea? Here are four ways to gain an advantage from a turndown.

1. Make Every NO an Opening, Not an Ending.

Even if someone rejects your idea today, it can be a networking opportunity for tomorrow. Very few people will flat out say, "Don't ever darken my doorstep again." In fact, chances are, if they're human, they're going to feel kind of bad for letting you down. Ask, "Would you mind if I let you know about my prog-ress in the future?" I guarantee, most people will say yes to that. Then follow through. Add them to your Rolodex, and keep in touch as your business grows.

2. Dig Beneath the NO.

Make the rejection an opportunity to do valuable research. Within every NO is a piece of information that will help you refine your pitch and your product. Instead of slinking out the door, stay in your seat for as long as they'll let you, and pick their brains. What do they know that you don't know about the business you're attempting to break into?

3. Don't Universalize a NO.

No product or service is right for everybody. If you get turned down, chances are you haven't refined your niche. Or maybe you've approached the wrong person. Before you leave the meeting, ask the person you pitched to if he or she can suggest others who might be interested in your product or service.

4. Get a YES the Next Time.

I've heard dozens of stories of successful entrepreneurs that kept going back, sometimes for years, re-knocking on that door. They have an unwavering "I'll show them" attitude.

DONNY'S DO: THE COLD CALL

Do you break into a cold sweat at the very thought of making a cold call? It's not a physical impediment. It's an emotional barrier, and you have to separate the consequences from real-life catastrophes. Psych yourself up by asking, "What is the worst thing that could happen?" The answer is not so scary: "They'll say no!" You won't die. You won't be dragged off to bad idea prison. You won't lose your shirt. You won't get sick. Maybe you'll have a moment of embarrassment or a week of disappointment—small prices to pay for realizing your dream.

Don't spend too much time wallowing. Get back on the horse. Pick up the phone and call the next person on your list.

CHAPTER 12

Saved by a
Big Idea

You're down to your last buck, living in the poorhouse, scraping the bottom of the barrel. Can you be saved by a big idea?

People never get tired of hearing the true comeback stories. What are the secrets of these people who used failure as a launching pad for success?

Launching from the Bottom

On so many occasions, the big idea that made millions was born of adversity. We had a guy on the show named Kaile Warren, a former contractor who created an amazing company called Rent-A-Husband. Kaile is a national success story, but he founded his company when his life had hit rock bottom. Kaile had run a small construction business for years, but when an accident forced him to close down, his debts began to mount. Ultimately, he lost everything. One night, Kaile, who was homeless, was sitting in an abandoned warehouse, at the end of his game, when an idea popped into his head: *Rent-a-Husband—*

for those jobs that never get done. Could he make a business of it? He thought, "I'm broke, I'm all alone, and I'm almost forty years old. What do I have to lose?"

How does a guy with nothing but the shirt on his back start a business? Kaile knew about a local support group for divorced women, and he paid it a visit with a handmade flyer that read: "Need a Husband? Obviously. Why not rent me?" He received more than fifty calls and his work caught the attention of local media. Not only was it

Big Idea Lesson: Kaile's story sounds miraculous, but he had to work for his miracle. The key is that he didn't roll over and go back to sleep. He didn't get up the next morning and say, "Who do I think I am?" He acted, taking one small step after another.

an inspirational story, it was a *great* idea.

Today, Kaile has a national franchise, he's written a book, and he is the home improvement correspondent for CBS. He was literally saved by a big idea.

Start with What You Know

Another inspirational guest on *The Big Idea* was Nadja Piatka, who now sits atop a twenty-million-dollar company, established through desperation and grit. Ten years ago, Nadja was a stay-at-home mom, happily married (she thought) to a dentist. They were experiencing a normal financial crunch, house mortgaged to the hilt, but getting by. Then one day Nadja's husband came home and announced that he'd met someone else, and Nadja's life changed dramatically.

With two kids, minimal child support, no income, no training, and no alimony, Nadja was in desperate straits. She remembers vividly the moment she hit bottom. A bill collector came to the house, and she instructed her daughter to crawl under a table with her so they couldn't be seen from the window. The humiliation was extreme, and the look on her daughter's face was even worse.

Nadja loved to cook, so she decided to take a stab at something she knew how to do—healthier versions of desserts. Then she started peddling them to local outlets, where her "brownies with a conscience" were a big hit. Her first big sale was a low-fat muffin to McDonald's Canada.

Years after Nadja Foods took off, when she was honored by the Foundation of Canadian Women Entre-

> **Big Idea Lesson:** Nadja envisioned success before she made it, believing that if she could picture her products anywhere, they could *be* there. She used to imagine her brownies sitting on the counter at Subway—and today they are.

preneurs as Entrepreneur of the Year, Nadja turned to her daughter and said, "Today, we're sitting *at* the table."

Take the Down Staircase Up

Dani Johnson is a success coach with thousands of clients, who advises some of the top CEOs in the country. That's pretty remarkable when you hear her story. Dani was abused as a child, pregnant at seventeen, and homeless at twenty-one. She was living out of her car when she decided that she was not going to be homeless anymore. She had nothing to build a business on—no phone, no business cards, no brochures, no receipts, not even a product. All she had was her personality and her determination. She figured that she could talk, so she talked a health products company into giving her a shot as a commission rep. They had nothing to lose; her income would be solely derived from her sales. Dani's office was a public phone booth, and she was good at her job. In a short period of time, Dani became the top sales producer for the company. And then she kept building on that success—eventually being sought after as a guru for others struggling to get a foothold.

Here are the success strategies Dani shared with us on *The Big Idea*:

1. Prepare for the marathon, not the sprint. When Dani first started hitting her stride, she was so focused on making millions that she forgot to take care of herself. After suffering a heart attack at twenty-four and a nervous breakdown at twenty-five, she realized that her goal had to be deeper than just going after the money—and she had to pace her dream.

2. Weigh ego with bank account. Dani noticed that many people she encountered in business had huge egos and tiny bank accounts. She learned to pay attention to those who had proven success, not those who talked big. She shadowed the winners to find out how they did it.

3. Prosper where you're planted. Show you can be trusted with the small things. Start with five employees and do it well, and you will grow to fifty employees.

4. Marketplace pays for value. People are loyal to people, not to products. If you establish a relationship with your customers, you will be recession proof.

5. Create results for others. Don't ask, "How much money can I make?" Ask, "Who can I create success for now?"

The big idea that saved Dani was not a product or service. It was Dani herself. Her ability to understand the way people are, and to appeal to them from the heart, rescued her. And now she is in the business of rescuing others.

DONNY'S DO: THE BOTTOMLESS
PIT OF POSSIBILITY

I can't tell you how many times I've heard stories from people who "hit bottom" and turned their lives around. Here's the secret: There *is* no bottom. It's almost like a religious belief—that you can be saved by a big idea. If you think you've hit bottom, scratch around in the soil. I guarantee you'll find another layer. Do you have what it takes to keep digging?

CHAPTER 13

Who Said It Was Too Late?

D o you think your time has passed—that the train left the station without you? Do you have more regrets than you have dreams?

As much as I enjoy seeing young kids full of fire who have made it, the greatest inspiration comes from those who decided in midlife to go for dreams that have been percolating since they were kids. The conventional wisdom is that as people get older they become more risk averse. I'm not convinced. I have seen too many people change their lives at forty, fifty, sixty, and beyond.

When I interviewed Joy Behar, the popular comedian and cohost of *The View*, a lot of viewers were surprised to learn that she didn't start doing standup comedy until she was forty. As she told me on the show, "Until I was forty, I did everything that was expected of me. I was a teacher because it was expected of me. I was a wife and mother because it was expected of me. But it was still not really enough. I had this other little voice inside, saying, 'You have to do what *you* want to do.' " And that's what she did—brilliantly, as it turns out.

It isn't just people who are actively dissatisfied with their careers who dream about change. You can work in a profession for decades, achieve great success, and enjoy what you do, and still get that itch to conquer a new challenge. That's what happened to me. When I decided to sell Deutsch, it was not because I had to sell. The agency was stronger than ever. But the passion that propelled me forward through the lean years just wasn't there anymore. It was like reading an exciting thriller and already knowing the ending. It diminishes the thrill. The irony of success is that you get to a place where you can be cocooned from the very thing you love the most—the fight. Most successful people just stay in their comfort zone. I wanted a new challenge where the ending was unknown.

I realize that not everyone has this need. Some people find new passion in their work every single day for a lifetime. Good for them. But because *The Big Idea* is focused on the dreamers and the risk-takers, I tend to see more of the type of people who make a daring leap. Driven by sheer passion, desperation, or sometimes both, they choose to accelerate when their peers are slowing down.

Midlife Crisis = Opportunity

You've heard the Chinese proverb that crisis equals opportunity. Take it to heart. In this rough economy, I've talked to many people who have lost their jobs or been downsized after twenty-five or thirty years in a company. They're hitting the marketplace at a terrible time, competing against people half their age and for half their salary. That's a crisis! Others have an inner crisis—they feel stuck at a job they hate, going through the motions until retirement. Is that any way to live? The difference between the person who sinks and the person who thrives is a gut recognition that their crisis is an opportunity.

Michael Gates Gill has got to be the poster boy for midlife transformation. He wrote about it in his best-selling book, *How Starbucks Changed My Life*, and he talked about his experience on *The Big Idea*. Michael is the real deal—the kind of story that makes everyone stop and consider what truly matters in their lives.

Michael was a member of the lucky sperm club. His father was the famed writer Brendan Gill, and Michael's childhood was one of incredible affluence. Out of college, he joined J. Walter Thompson because that was what he was expected to do, and he spent most of his career as a creative director, essentially sliding along, decade after decade, never questioning what he was doing or whether he loved it. In the process he grew stale, and people started to notice. When Michael was fifty-three, he was fired—a big blow, but not mortal. He figured he'd become a consultant, and he kept sliding along for another ten years, buttressed by a Rolodex full of contacts. But in his early sixties, the phones gradually stopped ringing, and Michael was scraping the bottom. His marriage collapsed, he was broke, and just when he thought it couldn't get worse, he was diagnosed with a rare brain disorder.

Sixty-three years old, with no health insurance and no prospects, Michael ducked into a Starbucks one day to soothe his misery with a latte. As fate would have it, they were having a hiring event, and someone asked him if he wanted a job. Desperation or wild courage—he's not sure which—led him to say yes. A big selling point was Starbucks' policy of providing health insurance to part-time workers.

And that, in a nutshell, was how Michael's life was saved—not just financially and physically, but mentally and emotionally. He found an environment where workers were treated with respect and loving kindness, where he was not judged on his family name or his fancy pedigree, but on his humanity and work ethic. Michael told us that stumbling into this new life was an uplifting experience. He said, "I'm happier today as a barista wearing a green apron than I ever was in a Brooks Brothers suit."

Is it really just that simple? It seems that way when you look

Big Idea Lesson: There are riches to be found when you step outside your comfort zone.

at Michael. He is not dejected, ashamed, depressed, or embarrassed. He actually seems grateful. It's absolutely authentic, and it has to give you pause. And by the way, in the process of finding himself, Michael discovered that he was a pretty great writer. His book became a huge best seller.

Riches to Rags and Back Again

As inspiring as rags-to-riches stories can be, the riches-to-rags-and-back-again stories like Michael's are just as compelling. Here's another one that will resonate with midlifers. Stephen Key hit fifty believing that the money spigot would never run out. He had developed a hot product, a special label called Spin-formation, and he'd sold three million labels in five years. His accountant told him he'd never be able to spend all the money—and Stephen took him at his word. He and his family spent wildly and saved little. Then one day, the business dried up, and Stephen went from millions to zero overnight. With three kids heading for college, he knew he had to get back on the horse, but what could he do?

Stephen's crisis became his opportunity. As he was desperately searching for a lifeline, one presented itself, in the form of a friend with an idea. Now, I have to stop here and point out that not everyone would have grabbed this particular concept and run with it—especially a fifty-something guy with absolutely no experience with the product or market. But Stephen did.

The idea was quite simple, yet completely unheard of—guitar picks designed and shaped in iconic ways. Stephen's first design was a skull. Would it work? Hard to know, since in the eighty-year history of guitar picks they had never strayed from the basic heart-shaped design. Stephen took drawings of his skull to music stores and asked the employees what they thought. They loved it. He took a skull pick to a trade show, and it worked instantly. Hot Picks was born. His grabbed the imagination of the industry by understanding his market—the cool kids.

Big Idea Lesson: You don't have to be young to be cool. Big ideas are *always* cool.

Encouraged by the early enthusiasm, Stephen went to town, eventually creating 150 designs. There are Mickey Mouse guitar picks, vampires, rock themes, and movie tie-ins. Just about any hot theme is fair game.

Four years after the launch, Hot Picks are selling briskly in ten thousand stores—including Wal-Mart, where they move at a rate of twenty thousand a day. And Stephen is relishing his new life. He's living proof that a big idea can happen at any age.

What's *Your* Second Life Story?

How do you recognize that the moment is right to write a new script? Marianne Williamson, the acclaimed lecturer and author whose spiritual perspective has inspired millions of people around the world, visited *The Big Idea* to share wisdom from her newest book, *The Age of Miracles: Embracing the New Midlife*. Marianne's goal is to turn midlife on its head. Most people think of growing older as a time of diminishing opportunities. She wants to reframe the second stage of life as a time of increasing possibilities.

This is an intriguing idea. I meet so many people my age or older who can't get past the mental block that the best years of their lives are over. They don't buy it that sixty is the new forty, or fifty is the new thirty. We all know these people. They like to talk about how the youth are squeezing them out, and they can be bitter about it. It always amazes me when some guy who was at the top of his field, capable of moving mountains, starts thinking like a victim once he hits fifty. If you want to break out of this self-ageism, you've got a lot going for you that the younger crowd can't beat. Your competitive edge rests in the following:

1. You've Been There, Done That.

Most of us can remember moments in our youth when we experienced a crushing failure or rejection, and thought, "I'll never recover from this." But we did, and even went on to view that moment as a defining part of our success. Young people don't have the advantage of hindsight to bring perspective to their struggles. You know you can overcome barriers because you've done it before. The end of the world is never the end of the world.

2. Your Toolbox Is Full.

No experience is ever wasted. No contact is ever irrelevant. Take a look at what you've accumulated over the years. Sit down and make a list of what's in your toolbox. What's your knowledge base, what have you done, who do you know?

3. You're Free to Invent.

It used to be that by the time you reached fifty, your kids were out the door and you had more freedom to change course. That's not so true anymore. I should know. I'm fifty and I have an infant daughter. Even so, there's a new form of creativity brewing among the baby boomers. The old images of retirement no longer seem so attractive. There's more freedom to reinvent your-self.

One of the most outstanding cases of reinvention I know is Jesse Ventura. In his fifty-one years, he's had more lives than a cat, each one remarkable and satisfying in a different way—Navy Seal, pro wrestler, actor, governor of Minnesota, author, television and radio host. What's impressive about Jesse is that, no matter how many different hats he wears, the core Jesse-ness is always there. He has mastered the art of pursuing opportunity without compromising his identity. He's also got that all-important quality—*attitude*.

It starts with attitude. It's a fact that others will tend to see you the way you see yourself. I've met old men who were thirty and young men who were sixty—the number on the page is no excuse. Colonel Sanders was sixty-five when he launched his chicken franchise business. It's never too late. Your train is sitting in the station, and it's up to you whether you'll get on board.

BIG IDEA TOOLBOX
RESOURCES FOR SECOND LIFERS

* The Service Corps of Retired Executives—SCORE (www .score.org): A resource partner of the Small Business Administration (SBA) dedicated to entrepreneur education and the formation, growth, and success of small busi-nesses nationwide.
* AARP (www.aarp.org): The organization for Americans over fifty.
* RetirementJobs.com (www.retirementjobs.com): Matches companies friendly to over-fifty workers with job seekers.

(continued)

* Workforce 50 (www.workforce50.com): An employment resource for older Americans.
* Retired Brains (www.retiredbrains.com): Connects older workers with employment and nonprofit opportunities.

DONNY'S DO: TEAR OFF THE REARVIEW MIRROR

If you're going to move forward, you can't be straining to look behind you. I don't care who you are, there is always a new horizon. The biggest mistake people make in midlife is to get caught up in the mentality that "I've got twenty years invested in selling insurance [or being a lawyer, or working at the post office]—how can I throw it away?" Everything you've done in the past contributes to the next possibility, but it only works if you're watching the road ahead.

Getting to Your
First Million

CHAPTER 14

From Zero to
Millions

am constantly struck by the consistency of the way businesses get started. You have a moment of inspiration, an idea. You sketch it at your kitchen table, cook it up on your stove, tinker in your garage. You create a product. If it's a gourmet food, you take it to a local gourmet store. If it's a clothing item, you take it to a small boutique. Times may have changed since the time of Andrew Carnegie and Henry Ford, but the essential formula for the American Dream remains the same. It's having a big idea, producing the result, and then pounding the pavement—either physically or virtually. That's how entrepreneurs everywhere go from zero to a million.

And guess what? You don't have to have a bundle to get started.

The $200 Windfall

Have you ever heard the saying "It takes money to make money"? That's not always the case, as I learned most vividly from the incredible Paula Deen. Paula, who has created a food empire, got her start with just two hundred dollars and some good old-fashioned Southern home cooking.

When you meet Paula Deen, your first thought is, "No wonder she's so successful—she's such a natural people person." That's why it's a shock to learn that Paula spent twenty years suffering from agoraphobia—literally frozen with fear at the idea of leaving her house. It wasn't until age forty-two, struggling financially and on the verge of divorce, that Paula had a wake-up call. She knew she had to take responsibility for her life so she could take care of her sons.

One thing Paula could do was cook, so with two hundred dollars she started a catering service, called The Bag Lady, that delivered homemade lunches to businesspeople at their offices. Her teenage sons, Jamie and Bobby, made the deliveries. Paula still remembers almost to the penny how she spent her two-hundred-dollar investment—fifty dollars for groceries, forty dollars for a cooler, and the remainder for a license and incidentals.

When Paula first started her catering company, working sixteen to twenty hours a day, she wasn't dreaming big dreams. Her goal was much more basic. "My idea of success," she often said, "was if we needed to go to the grocery store on Wednesday, we could do it and the check would not bounce." Sheer tenacity, hard work, and a product that kept people coming back for more, allowed Paula to grow. Within a couple of years, she was able to start a small restaurant, building steadily along the way.

How did Paula transform herself from a humble Savannah cook to an international phenomenon? What is the secret of Paula's success? Paula and her sons, Jamie and Bobby—who are now great cooks and entrepreneurs in their own right—have achieved international renown. They are an institution in Savannah, Georgia, where their restaurant, The Lady and Sons, is one of the hottest places to go for a good meal in the whole city. But the key seems to be something as old-fashioned as their cooking. When we had Bobby and Jamie on the show, they offered these Southern-style business tips:

1. **"Come on in and put your feet up."**—Business Translation: Make people feel welcome from the moment you meet them.

2. **"Dance with the one who brung ya."**—Business Translation: Be loyal to people who are loyal to you.

3. **"Much obliged."**—Business Translation: Never forget that a little gratitude goes a long way.

4. **"Don't get too big for your britches."**—Business Translation: Never show a hint of arrogance in life or in business.

5. **"Y'all come back now, y'hear?"**—Business Translation: Make sure your customers know they are a part of the family, and you hope to see them again real soon.

As for Paula, the woman you see today simply oozes charm. She grew into herself in the process of building a business. But first she had to reach down inside and find the courage and will to spend her last two hundred dollars to create possibilities for herself and her children.

Start a Business with $500

Paula's story is not as special as you may think. I'd like to bust the myth once and for all that you have to have a ton of money and a slew of investors to get off the ground. There are multimillion-dollar companies out there today that started with investments of less than five hundred dollars.

Wayne Perry discovered his big idea by accident. As a self-defense instructor in the 1990s, he taught people how to use pepper spray. His self-demonstration was a big hit on TV shows. When producers found out that he was willing to get sprayed in the face, they couldn't resist.

Wayne had suffered for years from cluster headaches, which were painful and debilitating. One day he felt a headache coming on just as a reporter was about to spray him. After the demonstration, he realized that his headache was gone. Intrigued, he did some research and learned that the active ingredient in pepper spray depleted the chemicals in the sinus that caused the headache. So he started to use his self-defense tool as a home remedy. That went on for eight years.

Big Idea Lesson: **All the money in the world won't make a difference if your idea is lousy. And all the poverty in the world won't stop you if your idea is great.**

In 2003, Wayne found himself out of work, a single dad with barely enough money to pay the rent. He decided to go for it. He took his last $350, mixed a batch of the spray in his kitchen, bottled it in nasal spray containers, and started selling Sinus Buster on eBay. He knew it was safe, because the spray used only natural ingredients. It was an instant hit. Today, Sinus Buster is FDA registered and is sold in chain health food and vitamin stores—and Wayne is making two million dollars a year.

Like Wayne, Kelly Flatley also started her company, Bear Naked Granola, in her kitchen. In college, Kelly had been famous for her all-natural fruit and nut granola. At age twenty-three, looking for a direction in life, she wondered if she could turn her talent into a business. Kelly started out with one hundred dollars—buying enough ingredients in bulk to make a ten-pound batch in her mother's kitchen. She packed it in plastic bags with raffia ties and called it Bear Naked Granola, to indicate that her product was pure and natural. Then Kelly hit the street, selling her product at sidewalk sales and a couple of small local markets. The response was positive enough to keep her going and to attract the interest of Kelly's childhood friend, Brendan Synnott. They decided to go into business together—which meant moving back into their parents' homes, and pounding the pavement every day, giving out free samples at community events and selling small batches to specialty and health food stores in their neighborhood. Every cent they earned went into the product.

Their big breakthrough came through a clever pitch idea. They decided to sell the Stew Leonard's buyer by serving him "breakfast in bed." But when they showed up at his office at 7:30 one morning holding their breakfast tray, they were told that the buyer was on vacation. Just as they were about to leave, Stew Leonard Jr. walked into the lobby. He was so intrigued that he agreed to take the meeting himself. Two hours later, he ordered fifty cases.

Today, Bear Naked Granola is a twenty-five-million-dollar company, with over two thousand retailers across the country—all started with a hundred-dollar batch in Kelly's kitchen.

Big Idea Lesson: **If you've got the goods, you'll make the sale.**

The final takeaway message from these stories and dozens like them: If you think your biggest obstacle is lack of capital, think again. Chances are you just haven't found the right concept or execution. Instead of beginning with the question "How much money will I need to start my business?" ask, "How can I get my business going with the five hundred or thousand dollars I have in savings?"

Don't Go for the Gold

If you aspire to be a great entrepreneur, you have to do it for the right reasons. Before you can even think about getting to your first million, you must decide what you're going to offer to your first customer. As Leslie Mayer, a senior fellow at the Wharton School and personal adviser to some of the top CEOs in the country, puts it, "Focus on the promise, not the prize." In other words, the payoff will come if you focus on giving your customers what they need and want. If you chase the money first, you'll be constantly off the mark.

You'll hear that same advice from such top guys as Warren Buffett and Donald Trump. You can say it's just a rich person's perspective, but it's also true. If money was the answer, every wealthy man and woman would be blissfully happy, and we know that's not the case.

A couple of years ago, Warren Buffett made headlines when he gave away the bulk of his fortune—thirty-seven billion dollars—to the Bill and Melinda Gates Foundation. Although he also gave his children substantial money for their charitable foundations, he made a point of saying he purposely didn't leave them a boatload of dough. "What do you think it would do for my kids if I gave each of them a billion dollars?" he asked. "They wouldn't have to work anymore or think anymore. It would wreck them."

I asked the Buffett kids if they're bitter about not getting a big windfall, and they just laughed. Bitter? They said they couldn't be more proud of their dad and what he did with his money. Their parents raised them to have perspective, vision, and drive of their own. And they like it that way.

You may fantasize about how wonderful it would be to inherit vast wealth, and never have to worry about money, but the sweet spot comes when you accomplish something yourself, and money is a tangible reward for your efforts. I've also interviewed Donald Trump's kids Ivanka and Donald Jr., and they speak with some pride about how their father always made it clear to them they would have to work for their money, and that included doing their fair share of menial jobs. They had many advantages as kids, including going to the best schools, but the rest was up to them. Both are now excelling. They're among the hardest working young professionals I've met. I've even had young Eric

Trump on the show; he's following in his family's very effective footsteps.

So, the lesson is twofold: Follow the path that you are passionate about and the money will follow you. And if you're a parent, don't rob your kids of the luxury of being hungry. It's something money can't buy.

Four Millionaire Shortcuts

Pick up almost any business advice book and you'll read some variation of the statement: "There's no such thing as an overnight success." I'd say it all depends on your definition of *overnight*. Can you go to bed at night and wake up the next morning a millionaire? Not likely, unless you bought the winning Powerball ticket. But what truly amazes and inspires me about so many successful entrepreneurs is the speed at which they rocketed to the top once they got their ideas in gear.

On *The Big Idea* we utilize the wisdom of successful entrepreneurs who went from zero to a million with remarkable speed. I asked a group of them to share the one piece of advice they would give to any new person starting out that would shortcut the process.

1. Claim the Spotlight.

Cameron Johnson, the author of *You Call the Shots*, and a regular on *The Big Idea*, believes that the key to quick success is simply to put yourself out there. He learned this at the tender age of eight, when he did just that. Cameron was a huge fan of the *Home Alone* movie and its child star, Macaulay Culkin. He desperately wanted to see the suite at the Plaza Hotel that was featured in the movie, and he begged his parents to take him there.

They struck a bargain—if he made straight A's for a year, they'd go to New York City. Cameron buckled down and got the grades. When he found out they'd be staying at the Plaza, he wrote a letter to Donald Trump: "Dear Mr. Trump, You probably don't know who I am. My name is Cameron Johnson, I'm eight years old, and the only thing I want is to see the suite where they filmed *Home Alone*." He addressed the letter to "Donald Trump, The Plaza, New York City," and mailed it, hoping it would find its destination. And he didn't tell his parents.

When the family arrived at the Plaza, the receptionist said, "You must be Cameron." As his surprised parents stared in amazement, the receptionist told him, "Mr. Trump arranged for you to stay in the suite for your entire visit. He appreciates so much your writing to him."

What a great lesson for a young kid. You can reach out to a powerful person and be taken seriously. Cameron learned it well, because by the time he was fifteen he had started three companies. His first, on the heels of the Plaza stay, was a greeting card business for family and friends, called Cheers and Tears, which he ran from his home computer. As a teenager, Cameron started a business providing scrolling ads for Web browsers, and made his first million before graduating from high school. He'd started twelve companies by age twenty-one.

Precociousness paid off for Cameron, but it's an essential step for any entrepreneur. Want to get advice from your business idol? Write a letter, just like Cameron did. Invite someone you admire in the field to lunch. Send a flattering e-mail. You can ask for what you need and be taken seriously.

2. Put a Stake in the Ground.

The vision comes first. John Assaraf, founder of OneCoach, a multibillion-dollar enterprise, didn't know how he was going to do it, but he set out his vision first. When he was twenty-two, John wrote down a goal that by the age of forty-five he'd have a net worth of three million dollars. He didn't have an exact plan. He was a high school dropout selling real estate at the time. But he put a stake in the ground and challenged himself. That was the key. Then he followed the steps.

It's important to put that stake in the ground—to name your vision. Yes, a business plan is important, but you don't have to wait to act until it is finalized. It's okay to start with an imperfect plan and dedicate yourself to perfecting it. Think of it as a creative process. In advertising, television, and other so-called "creative" endeavors, we learn that sometimes the greatest inspiration comes when you're already in the thick of it.

You learn by getting thrown into the deep end of the pool. That was true for me. By going into a small family business, I got a broad perspective early on. You learn lessons along the way. Each year you realize how little you knew the year before, and you keep improving.

3. Use Technology to Leap Ahead.

It's rare these days to meet an entrepreneur who isn't using the Internet in some way. But did you know that you could slash years off your climb by using it wisely? Laura Rowley, a *Big Idea* expert, writes a column for Yahoo Finance and is the author of *Money and Happiness: A Guide to Living the Good Life*. Laura advises that technology is the key to rapid growth, even if you're starting out with very little capital. Technology has changed everything. Look at low-cost technologies you can employ to run your business. In the old days, you'd advertise a business; now an e-mail blast can accomplish the same thing for nothing. You can reduce costs by outsourcing Web site design, graphic design, programming, bookkeeping, and other services you need for your business overseas. On sites like Elance.com and Guru.com, professionals bid to do your job. You can find quick help concierge services like GetFriday.com.

Laura suggests that start-up businesses build audiences first by blogging. The people who visit your site will become your first customers.

4. Team Up, Not Down.

There is a tendency when your company is just starting out to cling jealously to every aspect of a business, but it's the people you partner with who can make the crucial difference between being big or small. The smartest thing I ever did when I was building the agency was to make key people partners. Even if it's only three percent, when there's a sense of ownership, people are going to shine.

Another mistake many entrepreneurs make is that they hire people who are weaker versions of themselves, instead of choosing people who bring their own superior qualities to the business. Hire people who are smarter than you. If you can keep your ego in check, it becomes one of your greatest benefits. Your business can't grow if you're always thinking, "If I don't do it myself, it won't get done."

If inner drive is the first rule, the second rule is outer support. Gloria Mayfield Banks, the national sales director of Mary Kay Cosmetics, who fought her way to the top in the midst of great personal crisis, offered this wisdom: "It is important to take advice from people you are willing to exchange places with, not just people who offer advice. It's okay to be a copycat as long as you copy the right cat. Surrounding yourself with excellent powerful people who love what they do creates a success platform of excellence."

DONNY'S DO: BE MARKET SAVVY, NOT MARKET SHY

When you're facing a shaky market, the temptation is to be risk averse and put your dream on hold. So many people ask me, "Should I wait to start my business until the economy improves?" Not necessarily.

Cynthia Kersey, head of the aptly named Unstoppable Enterprises, Inc., put this notion into words for me. She said, "Fact is the enemy of truth." In other words, the fact might be that the market is down. But that's not the determining truth of your business. Companies like Microsoft and Hewlett-Packard were started during recessions, and they thrived because they met specific demands. You can take advantage of consumers' budget consciousness by finding a way to provide something cheaper. A down market can also be a benefit in calculating business expenses. Suppliers may be more competitive in pricing because they're hurting, too. A struggling marketplace forces you to think more creatively than ever, and that's a good thing.

On *The Big Idea* we've found that when the economic news is bad, people get more inspired to do their own thing. They don't want to wait for the market to piss away their money, or for their companies to crumble. They want to grasp control of their own fate. We make it possible for people to say, "I have two thousand dollars in the bank. Instead of investing it in the stock market, I can invest in myself."

CHAPTER 15

Fueled by Mom
Power

Moms rule. Some of the most innovative and driven entrepreneurs we've had on the show are moms on a mission. They're motivated to make life better, easier, saner for their families. These successful mompreneurs have obliterated the conflict between working and stay-at-home moms. Owning their own businesses has allowed them to have it all without sacrificing what they love most. They've found ways to be there for their kids and run successful businesses, starting at their own kitchen tables.

If you're a mother (or a father, for that matter) who longs to be more present to your family while also pursuing your career, listen up.

Mothers of Invention

As a parent, you've got a skill that is invaluable in any business, and you may not even know it. Major companies spend fortunes finding people who do what you do as a matter of course every day—you solve problems. Almost every successful business we've featured that was started by a mom came from a very basic problem that they were driven to solve.

Tamara Monosoff, CEO of Mom Inventors, Inc., is in the business of helping bring mom-invented products to market. But if you'd asked her ten years ago what she would be doing, she never would have imagined herself in this role. Back then she lived in Washington, D.C., working as a presidential appointee to the Clinton administration at the White House and the U.S. Department of Education. When she and her husband moved back to California after the birth of her first daughter, Tamara didn't want to put an end to her work life. She'd always loved working, and she sought creative pursuits that would allow her to be close to her baby.

She found her opportunity when her daughter reached the toddler stage. It came through her effort to solve one of the most mundane but irritating things in the world—the fascination little ones have with unraveling toilet paper from the roll. Tired of having reams of toilet paper littering the bathroom, Tamara looked for a gadget that would save her toilet paper, and failing to find one, she decided to invent it. She sketched her concept for TP Saver, modeling it after a hair-permanent rod that could slide into the corner of a toilet paper roll and snap into place without removing the roll. She was then lucky to find a manufacturer who offered to make a prototype for a hundred dollars.

In the process of launching her product, Tamara was looking at the big picture—how to help moms like herself create success with their inventions. She built an umbrella company, Mom Inventors, Inc., and has become a key player in the mompreneur market.

Tamara grasped the central reality that necessity is the mother of invention. We've often had moms on *The Big Idea* who solved ordinary problems with inventive solutions.

Debbee Barker's daughters were her inspiration for FlipFOLD, the Ultimate Laundry Organizer. Their clothes were always piled on the floor, or shoved into closets and drawers in a wrinkled mess. And when they wanted something, they could never lay hands on it. Debbee pleaded with them, "Girls, when you do your laundry, fold clothes neatly and to the same size. Your rooms will be more organized with less clutter; your clothes will be neat and wrinkle-free." Her daughters replied that folding clothes was too hard and took too long. Debbee realized that they needed a laundry organizer to help them with the folding.

Debbee started thinking about the challenges of folding clothes. She had a little experience in that department. As a retail buyer, she'd seen how many business resources got wasted in the task. Retailers and manufacturers spend countless hours on organizing clutter and folding clothes for store presentation and shipping. Folding is a business expense not only in dollars but also in customer service. She realized that this versatile folding tool could do more than just help her kids. It could benefit many different businesses in the garment industry. Instead of devoting hours to folding clothes just so, employees could concentrate on helping customers.

Big Idea Lesson: By combining what she'd witnessed in business with what she experienced at home, Debbee found a product that fit a personal and professional need. Two markets for the price of one.

She cut out her original patent from a cardboard box and taped it together with duct tape. The result: a simple series of folding edges that produces a perfectly folded T-shirt every time. She marketed it as FlipFOLD, the Ultimate Laundry Organizer. Today, Debbee Barker's FlipFOLD is not only in millions of homes, it's a big part of the commercial laundry and dry cleaning business. Debbee Barker made it happen, and in the process created a great business opportunity for herself and her family.

Stories like Tamara's and Debbee's fill our in-boxes at *The Big Idea*, and we've featured many of them on the show—Pump

It Up, an inflatable "bouncy" party system for kids created by Brenda Dronkers, a stay-at-home mother of three, which has turned into a seventy-million-dollar business; or Boogie Wipes, created by two moms, Mindee Doney and Julie Pickens, who were tired of chasing runny-nosed toddlers around the house trying to get their noses clean. These mothers of invention, and thousands like them, are finding ways to build their nest eggs without leaving the nest. I applaud them.

BIG IDEA TOOLBOX
RESOURCES FOR MOMPRENEURS

* Mom Inventors, Inc. (www.mominventors.com): Tools and resources for inventing moms.
* *The Mom Inventors Handbook: How to Turn Your Great Idea into the Next Big Thing*, by Tamara Monosoff.
* *Mommy Millionaire: How I Turned My Kitchen Table Idea into a Million Dollars and How You Can, Too*, by Kim Lavine.
* *Mom's Business Magazine* (www.momsbusinessmagazine .com): A guide for home businesses.
* Moms in Business Network (www.mibn.org): A national network dedicated to supporting working mothers and their businesses.
* The Mom Pack (www.mompack.com): Moms promoting moms.
* *Mompreneurs: A Mother's Practical Step-by-Step Guide to Work-at-Home Success*, by Patricia Cobe and Ellen H. Parlapiano.
* Mompreneurs Online (www.mompreneursonline.com): A resource for work-at-home moms.

Moms Together

Moms have another advantage—a ready-made community of like-minded, resourceful friends who have similar needs. They form an automatic niche market. As an added bonus, I've always found that women are great at collaboration. Time and again, I've seen women put their heads together to form businesses that turn their informal conversations into multimillion-dollar ideas.

Daven Tackett was a stay-at-home mom in Tulsa, Oklahoma, a job she loved. But without a second income, she was always looking for ways to stretch the family budget. One of the most persistent problems she faced was how quickly kids grow out of clothing, which needs to be replaced. A couple of times a year she would hold garage sales to raise extra cash and recycle her kids' slightly worn clothes. She'd use the proceeds to buy new items. One day, Daven's friend Shannon Wilburn called her with an idea that she immediately knew was a home run—hosting consignment sales where people would sell their used items in larger groups. They tested the plan on seventeen friends from their church, inviting them to bring their gently used children's clothing and items to Shannon's home for a sale. The contributors would receive seventy percent of the price.

Daven and Shannon clipped threads, ironed clothing, hung them, and tagged them with prices. Their two-day sale netted them two thousand dollars, a result that thrilled them. But more exciting was the buzz. Suddenly, they were inundated with requests for new sales, and that's how their business took off. For their second sale, they moved from Shannon's living room to a three-car garage. The third sale occurred at a church gym. They named their business Just Between Friends—which captures the personal spirit of their enterprise.

With demand growing, they booked a room at a large event center in Tulsa, and it was packed. It soon became apparent that this was an idea with national potential. Friends, family, and perfect strangers from other cities had heard about them and wanted to host their own sales, and business friends encouraged them to franchise their concept. They had no idea what they should do first, so they found a franchise lawyer to help them, registered their name, and set up a Web site. They started selling franchises in January 2004, and now have sixty-one sales events in sixteen states.

Big Idea Lesson: Just Between Friends has succeeded because Daven and Shannon tapped into a family community that had a shared need.

The Mommy Millionaire

Kim Lavine had a big idea—and then she made it bigger. In 2000, Kim was a stay-at-home mother of two in Michigan, trying to make ends meet. Her husband had just lost his job, and she knew she had to find some way to help pay the bills. The opportunity came by accident when she was looking for a holiday gift she could make for her children's teachers. Her husband, who had been feeding deer in their backyard, carried the bag of corn feed into the house and left it next to Kim's sewing machine. When she saw it there, she suddenly had an inspiration. Using the corn as filler, she sewed several colorful fabric cases and called her invention the Wuvit. These healing pillows could be frozen or heated in the microwave to ease aching joints. It was such a big success at school that soon people were calling her, wanting to know where they could get Wuvits. Kim began selling her Wuvits at shopping mall kiosks, and was amazed to find that she could make a living with her popular product. By 2004, she was selling in high-end chains like Saks. Today her company does ten million dollars in business—and she has written a book about it, called *Mommy Millionaire*. Kim came on *The Big Idea* to give advice to homebound moms about how they can get started with a point and a click. Her advice is direct and practical, and it can all be done without leaving the house.

+ *It's easy to write a business plan, utilizing a Web site called score.org. The site provides a template—you just fill in the blanks. With this service you'll find out what to do every day for the first year.*
+ *Get a provisional patent from USPTO.gov, for under a hundred dollars. You'll be protected for a year while you get up and running.*
+ *Research manufacturers and suppliers by Googling your category or go to Thomasnet.com.*
+ *Start your own Web site through an online service such as Godaddy.com for seven dollars.*
+ *Get free press. For forty dollars, you can post a press release at Prweb.com, and they'll even help you write it. (The last time Kim did it, she got 60,000 hits and was inundated with calls from feature editors wanting to do stories.)*

Kim has done something I often see with successful entrepreneurs—she's passed it on. With her book and her outreach to other moms, she's on a mission to make the dream come true for others just like her.

DONNY'S DO: KITCHEN TABLE WISDOM

So, you're sitting in your kitchen in Denver, Wichita, Allentown, Tacoma—or Anywhere USA, thinking about how you can do what you love most, being a mom, and make some cash in the process. Are you a mommy millionaire in the making? Apply some kitchen table wisdom and take these steps:

1. It starts with a problem. Is something bugging you that you think you can find a way to fix?

2. Next step—coffee klatch. Talk it over with a few friends and create a support network.

3. Go shopping. Research the outlets that might carry a product such as yours. Look for similar concepts. Study the way items are packaged and priced. Take notes.

4. Do it. Start at your sewing machine, kitchen table, or garage. Invite others to join you. Put the kids to work. Family fun can become family riches.

CHAPTER 16

All in the
Family

My proudest moment in television was having my own dad on *The Big Idea*. I wanted to tell the world how much I owed this man, whose shoulders I stand on every day. But I got pretty choked up when he told me—and my viewers—"One of the best things that ever happened in my life was you coming to work for me. I discovered a dimension to you that I never would have discovered. It bonded us, and I'm so grateful." What an emotional moment. And it's true—my dad and I found each other through work.

Now, don't get the idea that our working relationship was one big *kumbaya* moment. We locked horns a lot. Our styles were like yin and yang. But we shared a common love for the business. My happiest memories are of walking over to the Oyster Bar at Grand Central Station after work, where we'd talk about the business over heaping plates of cherrystone pan roasts.

The biggest favor my dad did for me was to give me the freedom to run. He didn't sit around the office, wringing his hands and waiting for me to fail. He let me try things that he would never have tried, and when I succeeded, he was prouder than I was—and showed it. He doesn't hesitate to give me credit for making Deutsch a huge success, and I never stop giving him credit for doing the hard part of creating a platform of excellence and stability that made growth possible.

Not every family business has such a happy ending. Love and ego can be a combustible combination, erupting in feuds, power clashes, and even lawsuits. But that being said, the family business is the most reliable success formula in our nation's history. What's more gratifying than creating a legacy for generations to come—and doing it *your* way? The names are iconic—from Ford to Levi Strauss, family businesses have been the bedrock of our economy. Even today, about 90 percent of all companies in America are family-owned.

Look into any old family business and you'll find a core of wisdom that sometimes gets lost in today's strip-and-flip business culture. I had Todd Simon of Omaha Steaks on the show. Omaha Steaks was started by Todd's great-great-grandfather, a Latvian immigrant seeking his fortune on the American frontier. He and his son arrived at Ellis Island in 1898 and headed west, where they worked as butchers before opening their own company. In the 1940s, when Omaha became a hub for Union Pacific Railroad, they graduated to serving national customers, sending their meat to groceries and restaurants across the country. Their best advertisement was the railroad itself, which served their steaks in its dining cars. In every generation, Omaha Steaks found its opportunity for growth. Today, the company is best known for its phenomenal mail order business, making it the largest dry ice user in the country, and bringing in over four hundred million dollars a year.

Big Idea Lesson: Old-fashioned values are the hottest commodity in the modern marketplace. If you can offer Grandpa's quality and service to your customers, they'll salivate for more.

Omaha Steaks' fortunes were made not only by providing a product of unparalleled quality, but by holding fast to a winning philosophy. As Todd put it, "We are not in the steak business, we're in the love business." Nothing says love like a beautifully prepared meal or gift, and Omaha Steaks has cornered that market.

A Winning Formula

Another longtime family business we featured on *The Big Idea* was Enterprise Rent-A-Car. CEO Andy Taylor came on the show to talk about the company his father started in St. Louis in the 1950s, and how he dared to go up against the big boys, Hertz and Avis. He had a new concept—a car rental company that was locally based, not in airports, and that provided a service that was totally unique—picking up and dropping off customers at their homes. Fifty years later, Enterprise leads the industry, with nine billion dollars in revenue and 900,000 vehicles. All started by an entrepreneur with a vision of customer service. Jack Taylor started his company on a shoestring. Andy remembers his dad coming home and saying, "Take care of your clothes, Andy, because I can't afford to replace them."

Andy worked in his dad's business, starting at the bottom washing cars when he was sixteen. After he graduated from college, he took an entry-level position at RLM Leasing, a Ford Motor Company affiliate in San Francisco, to gain experience. In 1973, he returned to St. Louis and began his career at Enterprise.

Andy credits his father, now retired, for establishing healthy ground rules for their father- son interactions. The first was that no matter how much they disagreed behind closed doors, when they walked out they were going to present a united front. The second was that they weren't

Big Idea Lesson: This is the genius of family businesses—the ability to create and pass on a set of core values that doesn't waver from generation to generation.

going to talk about family issues at the office. Jack Taylor passed on a great company to his son. And the most valuable thing Andy inherited was a company culture that was focused on the field. "The employees aren't there to satisfy me," Andy said. "I am there to empower the field. I am serving them."

Ancestral Secrets

What's in your attic? You may not know. Attics are famous repositories of stuff you never see again. A mover once told me that, nine times out of ten, when people moved from one house to another, the contents of the attic were untouched from their last move. But on *The Big Idea*, we bring on people who climbed the stairs, brushed off the cobwebs, and found ancestral treasures waiting for them—treasures worth millions.

Instead, Jim Koch found the secret to his future success amongst the family relics in his parents' attic. Jim was part of a long tradition. Five generations of Koch men had been brewmasters, but the tradition seemed to have died as the popular interest in full-flavored beers had waned. But when Jim discovered an old family recipe from the 1800s, for Louis Koch Lager, he had an inspiration.

What had been going on in the U.S. beer industry for decades had really taken all of the allure out of working as a brewmaster. The big, mass-production breweries had reduced the role of the brewmaster from being the most important person in the business to being a supervisor who filled out personnel charts and dealt with union grievances.

Jim Koch's grandfather once told him, reminiscing about the good old days, "The owner of the brewery would make an appointment to see *me*." In the Old World breweries, the brewmaster had been treated as though he were a Teutonic god. That role didn't exist anymore.

One day, looking through a trunk in his parents' attic, Jim came across some yellowed papers, and had a big "Aha!" moment. Jim decided that he was tired of the big beer companies, and he wanted to make a "gourmet" product.

With his great-great-grandfather's recipe for Louis Koch Lager, and a determination to hand-craft quality, flavorful beer, Jim brewed his first batch of Samuel Adams Boston Lager in his kitchen in 1984. He chose the name in honor of the Boston patriot Samuel Adams, who had also been a brewer.

"I'll never forget tasting the first batch of Sam Adams," Jim recalled. "That was a magical moment. Realizing this was something that had one hundred and twenty years of family history behind it, something that nobody had tasted in a century—that was really cool."

Jim carried his bottled brew from bar to bar, and the bartenders themselves were his first focus groups. They loved it. But how did Jim take that tiny local success and make his first million? Contracting with a Pittsburgh brewery for a percentage of the business, Jim sold over five hundred barrels in his first year. That single business decision—to partner up with a reliable brewery—was a winner for Jim. And the brewery that took a gamble on a new kind of beer made millions, too. Today, this three-hundred-million-dollar business brews well over one million barrels a year.

> **Big Idea Lesson:** It's all about quality. Jim Koch's dad used to tell him, "No matter how good the marketing is, somebody's got to drink it." Jim put his entire focus into giving people a great-tasting glass of beer, and it paid off.

Jim's recipe and initiative hit the market at the beginning of a huge boom in microbreweries. His idea took hold at exactly the right time, with the craft beer boom of the eighties.

Boss, Mentor, Mom

June and Rochelle Jacobs are a great case study for the modern family business. We enjoyed having them on *The Big Idea* because they were so brutally honest about their battles, but also had a loving bond that was unmistakable. They reminded me a lot of the tensions and rewards I experienced working with my dad.

June Jacobs started the June Jacobs Spa Collection when she was a struggling single mother looking for a business opportunity. Working for a plastic surgeon, she noticed a void in the spa market for a line of luxurious botanical skin care products, and she started her company to address a very narrow niche market of high-end spas.

Enter Rochelle, her beloved daughter. When Rochelle sat down and talked to her mom about joining the business, she approached it like a combination business proposition and job interview, complete with a PowerPoint presentation. Rochelle had a vision—growing the June Jacobs Spa Collection from an eight-employee mom-shop to a multimillion-dollar company. June was so impressed, she agreed to bring Rochelle on board.

Big Idea Lesson: A younger generation can bring new fire and growth to an established business, but the core values have to be unwavering.

Today, the June Jacobs Spa Collection has one hundred and fifty employees and an international reputation.

June and Rochelle cheerfully admit that they "agree on absolutely nothing," making their working relationship one of constant (though healthy) friction. What makes it work is a foundation of common values, and a couple of clear, unbending rules—mostly designed to separate business from family life.

Family First, Then the World

The birth of Rachel and Andy Berliner's daughter, Amy, in 1987 coincided with the birth of a big idea. You could say they were in the business of nurturing, because that's what Amy's Kitchen was all about for them.

The Berliners didn't set out to make millions. They didn't dream of becoming the nation's leading natural frozen food brand, which they are today. Rachel and Andy just wanted to come up with a business that would support a relatively modest lifestyle, while providing delicious, healthy vegetarian food to others who shared their taste—but were often too busy to cook from scratch.

They started on a shoestring, using their own house and barn as headquarters. They borrowed money from family, and sold their car. Their first client was a local bakery that asked them to make a vegetarian pot pie.

The challenge of creating standard frozen food was beyond them. So what did they do? Andy called Swanson's and asked, "How do you make a frozen pot pie?" They actually told him! It was their first product, and it was such a hit that it outgrew the bakery.

When they decided to start producing the pot pie themselves, Andy and Rachel knew they needed a bank loan, but that was an uphill battle. Finally, a little bank that was new to their community agreed to loan them twenty thousand dollars. The loan officer, the kind of visionary that's hidden away in banks across the country, told the loan committee, "Someday the Berliners are going to be our best customer." And today they are.

The first two years were rough, but every day was an inspiration. "Our juice was hearing from our customers," Rachel told me. As they added products, the company began to take off, selling first in health food stores, and then expanding to regular supermarkets. Today Amy's Kitchen has revenues of $240 million a year.

When Rachel and Andy appeared on *The Big Idea*, they flew their own plane from California. But they don't look like high rollers. The same quiet spirit that launched an empire is still with them today. The key: They love what they do. Over the years, many big companies have wanted to buy the business, but they've never had any interest in selling. "We're a service business," Rachel said. "We like feeding people. Many of our customers have special needs that might not get met if a big company took over."

Big Idea Lesson: **Amy's Kitchen exploited the number one emotional advantage of a family business—the ability to build a customer base through personal trust and confidence.**

They're going to keep it in the family, and Amy herself, now a student at Stanford University, is fine with that. Amy is very much a part of the business and is often present at decision-making discussions. During the summer she likes to go to the plant and work on the burrito packaging lines. And, of course, she serves Amy's Pizza to her friends.

The New Family Business Model

Unlike previous generations, there isn't an automatic assumption that the kids are going to follow Mom and Pop into the family business. And even when family businesses plan for a smooth line of succession, things don't always work out. Just ask Steve Swindal, the son-in-law and heir apparent to George Steinbrenner's Yankees. When George's daughter filed for divorce, it effectively ended Swindal's future with the team. Only about one-third of all family businesses survive the transition to a second generation. For the most part, you can't hand it over to

Junior just because you're related. But if your goal is to keep a family business alive and thriving, it's not just going to happen by osmosis. Prepare for the pitfalls and exploit the advantages.

You'll have greater success bringing in a second generation if you follow these five family-friendly strategies:

FIVE KEYS TO A HAPPY FAMILY BUSINESS:

1. Put family first. If your business is going to cause upheaval in the family, just don't do it. It's not worth destroying your most important relationships. Successful family businesses learn to separate family and work. They don't discuss business at the dinner table. Likewise, if your sons, daughters, or other family members aren't as passionate about the business as you are, don't pressure them to join.

2. Set clear expectations and roles. Make sure to spell out exactly where everyone stands—especially if there are multiple siblings involved. Put roles and responsibilities in writing. It's not necessarily something you do at home, but you must do it in the office.

3. Set a high standard. In some ways, you have to make it harder on the next generation than on other employees. Your staff has to see them working in the trenches, or they'll never have their respect. Don't bring in your sons and daughters as executive vice presidents before they've learned the ropes. Donald Trump always started his kids at the bottom, and he was tougher on them than anyone.

4. Allow for change. Within your overall value system, allow the next generation to do things differently. Let them explore their future vision. That's how family businesses grow.

5. Give them their own turf. A very smart way to allow second generation growth while maintaining your core business is to give your sons or daughters a niche of their own. For example, my father's agency did print advertising. My niche was television. I was enabled to grow the business without stepping on anyone's toes. Donald Trump's father did the same thing. His arena was middle-class housing in Queens. Donald forged new territory in Manhattan.

DONNY'S DO: EXPRESS YOUR PRIDE

It cracked me up when June Jacobs admitted that she rarely praised her daughter, Rochelle, to her face because "I don't want her to get a swelled head"—although she bragged about her to others. I've seen that a lot in family businesses, and I guess it's an extension of dynamics that were set in place from the early years. Sometimes parents forget that their highly successful adult children aren't still fifth graders.

But there's also a dynamic in many families where the love and respect is just taken for granted. They may praise their other employees to the hilt, but forget to give their relations a slap on the back for a job well done. My advice to people who employ family members in their business—don't forget to tell them you appreciate them and are proud of them. It means a lot.

CHAPTER 17

People
to People

Behind every great idea is a human story. If you can find a way to tell it to the world, the sales will follow. On *The Big Idea*, we're attracted to great stories. It often happens that we're drawn in by the story first, before we even check out the product. That's how we found Michele Hoskins.

Talk about an all-American story. This lady has the goods. She is one of the most empowering guests we ever had on the show.

Michele's great-grandmother was a slave. She also made a fantastic pancake syrup. After she was emancipated, the recipe was passed down through the generations. And here was her great-granddaughter on my show, talking about how she's taken this recipe and made a fifty-million-dollar business out of it. It doesn't get any more inspirational than that.

Here's the thing about Michele's great-grandmother's recipe: It was a secret, passed down only to the third daughter. Since Michele wasn't a third daughter, she never got the recipe. But when she gave birth to her own third daughter, her mother parted with it.

When Michele started mixing up batches in her kitchen, she was a struggling single mother and schoolteacher, with no idea about becoming an entrepreneur. There were no African American mentors she could call on. But, as Michele told us, when she was a child her parents always said, "Anything the mind can conceive can be achieved." And that knowledge gave her the courage to start a business with no capital and no experience. She sold her car and condo, packed up the kids, and moved back in with her mother.

When Michele first started, she'd make syrup in the basement and haul it around to retail merchants, where she'd offer them a win-win proposition. If they sold the product, she'd come back later and invoice them. Then she'd go back and buy it herself—and ask her friends to do the same. Before long she didn't have to be a stealth customer. *Real* customers loved it.

Michele's big break came nine years into the business when she scored a three-million-dollar contract with Denny's. But it took two years of persistence to make it happen. Michele's angle was diversity. In the early 1990s, Denny's was facing lawsuits over discriminatory practices. Every day for two years, Michele called them

Big Idea Lesson: A great story plus a great product equals marketing success.

at the exact same time with the exact same message: "I know you're having problems with diversity. You need to talk to me. I can help." She finally got past the switchboard and talked to a live decision maker. In 1994, she became one of Denny's first minority- and women-owned suppliers. Once again, she created a win-win situation for the buyer.

Twenty years into the business, Michele's Syrup brings in fifty million dollars a year and she runs her own manufacturing plant. For her, it's all about creating family success—a moving concept for the great-granddaughter of slaves. As Michele put it, "I want to leave my daughters a business, not just a recipe."

What's *Your* Story?

The take-home message is simple: If you want to get your big idea in front of the masses, make news. You can toss the ad budget if your story is intriguing enough to hit the editorial pages. It may surprise you to hear this from an old ad guy, but free media is way more valuable than advertising because it creates an aura of credibility that you just can't buy. Besides, when you're just starting out and have very little money, traditional advertising isn't going to be available to you.

Think about it. There are thousands of newspapers, magazines, news and lifestyle TV shows, radio broadcasts, and Web sites, and they're all looking for stories. Why not yours? If your business has a great angle, or your personal journey is unique or intriguing, there are media outlets looking for you.

Earlier we talked about Fred DeLuca and the business success story of Subway. But the event that kicked Subway into the stratosphere was the story of Jared Fogle. Jared was a college student who created his own "Subway Diet," consisting of a six-inch turkey sub for lunch, and a foot-long veggie sub for dinner. After three months on the diet, he had lost nearly one hundred pounds, and gained some local notoriety. When news of Jared's diet reached the attention of Subway's marketing department, they decided to make Jared a spokesman, thus launching one of the most successful ad campaigns in fast-food history. Jared captured the public imagination in a way that conventional ad appeals could never do. I guarantee, for every ad dollar Subway spent on the campaign, they got triple the free publicity back.

Desiree Gruber, a *Big Idea* expert, knows a lot about getting free media. Desiree is one of the most successful public relations pros in the business, with fifteen years under her belt. Desiree has good advice for new companies looking for media coverage. "When people try to get into the media, they tend to want to look smart and cool, but the truth is that the media is looking for the story behind the product," Desiree says. "People want a story that they can relate to. People can't relate to super geniuses, nor do they want to, and when the product is more relatable, it is easier to understand." The short of it, Desiree says, is to be yourself and let your image and story make people want to be a part of your passion and your product. Her three essentials to helping your business develop self-fulfilling PR are:

1. **Have a great idea. No great business is without one.**
2. **Have a passion that people can relate to. Don't portray yourself as an immortal and unrivaled genius.**
3. **Have a news hook—something that's unusual, eye-catching, or simply newsworthy. Don't be afraid to show your true colors, your troubles, and your humanity.**

BIG IDEA TOOLBOX
FREE PUBLICITY RESOURCES

* PRWeb.com (www.prweb.com): A press release writing and distribution service on the Web.
* PublicityHound.com (www.publicityhound.com): A how-to site for publicizing your business.
* Publicity Insider (www.publicityinsider.com): A publication for PR-hungry businesses.
* *Free Publicity: A TV Reporter Shares the Secrets for Getting Covered on the News*, by Jeff Crilley.

It's Not About the Clothes

Nadine and Corinne Purdy have created three shops in Manhattan called Purdy Girl. Very cute idea, fashionable styles, and the potential to become a national business. But that's not what got these sisters onto *Oprah*, *Dateline NBC*, or *The Big Idea*. The price of admission to high-power publicity was their story—and it wasn't so pretty.

Corinne Purdy will never forget opening up the *New York Times* on a Sunday morning in 1996 and finding a feature about her older sister, Nadine. "Descent of a Woman," by Rene Chun, told of Nadine's fall from being a wife, mother, and business owner to a woman of the streets. Nadine was once the owner of Yoshi, the hottest boutique in New York, bringing in more than two million dollars a year. But Nadine took a wrong turn on the road to success, which culminated in a heroin addiction, prostitution, and homelessness. She lost everything, including her three children. And although her loyal sister Corinne helped as much as she could, the situation felt hopeless.

For Corinne, the most heartbreaking line in the *Times* article was Nadine's declaration that "When I'm healthy, I'm going to open another store with my sister." It broke Corinne's heart. She wanted to believe in her sister, but she couldn't imagine that day would ever come.

But it turned out that the *Times* feature, which seemed like a source of shame and despair, was really an opportunity. As Corinne sat in her apartment that morning, the phone rang. The caller introduced himself as Jim Abernathy from the Caron Foundation, an alcohol and drug treatment facility in Wernersville, Pennsylvania. He told Corinne that he had been so touched by her sister's story that he wanted to offer Nadine a full scholarship to stay at his facility.

That call was the beginning of a very long journey of recovery. From that time, the media continued to follow the story of

Big Idea Lesson: Thanks to media attention, Corinne and Nadine Purdy had plenty of people rooting for them when they opened their first store. Their moving human story brought customers. Everyone wanted to see a happy ending.

two sisters sticking together through thick and thin, facing the obstacles of drug addiction, having everything, losing everything, having a dream and building that dream together from the ground up. Today, Corinne and Nadine are successful entrepreneurs who built their business from a foundation of hard luck.

Become a Household Name

How many times a day do you use a product that has become a household name? Probably hundreds. Consider how many brand names have come to identify an entire category: You request Coke, not cola. You take a Tums, not an antacid. You ask for Sweet'n Low, not a sugar substitute. You Google someone, you don't search for them. Those lucky brands own their categories. We've seen a few on the show. Take the Taser.

Tom and Rick Smith were always fascinated by sci-tech creations, but their innovative drive really kicked in when they set out to solve a simple problem—protecting their mother. When she started talking about buying a gun for personal security, they thought, "Whoa, don't want Mom packing a deadly weapon." How could they use science as a nonlethal method of protection?

Trying to find a middle ground in self defense, Tom and Rick were inspired by their favorite TV show, *Star Trek,* and always wanted to make a real taser, so they started researching the idea. A taser-like device had actually been developed in the 1970s by John Cover, a scientist for the Apollo moon landing. But Cover's invention had limited use because it utilized gunpowder. The first thing Tom and Rick did was track down Cover himself. Now in his seventies, Cover agreed to work with them to develop a prototype for their safer, more user friendly design.

In 1991, the brothers launched Taser International. Their father took money out of his retirement account to fund the venture. Pretty early on they realized that their target audience was not going to be ordinary citizens—yet. First they had to get law enforcement on board. In the years since its start, Taser has gained wide use among law enforcement agencies—over eleven thou-

Big Idea Lesson: Taser met a real professional need, but Tom and Rick made it a household name by tapping into the civilian desire for protection.

sand police, correctional, and military agencies utilize it. In effect, they narrowed their market in order to expand it. And now they have also achieved the breakthrough in personal security they wanted for their mom. Taser is legal in forty-three states, and about 150,000 devices have been sold to citizens.

Today, this household name has revenues topping sixty-seven million dollars a year and trades on the NASDAQ under the trading symbol TASR.

Build Your Network

The take-home message is that it's all about people. The people you know, the people you want to know, and the people you hope will get to know you. Sometimes entrepreneurs have a tendency to keep their noses so close to the grindstone that they lose sight of the business benefits of networking.

Cynthia Good of *PINK* magazine noticed that her hardworking staff usually liked to eat lunch at their desks—a real sign of commitment and industriousness. She had to push her partner,

Genevieve, out the door one day to attend a luncheon for women in business. It would have been easy to skip the luncheon; there was so much to do. But wouldn't you know, at that luncheon Genevieve met the CMO of Guardian Insurance, who agreed to sponsor a section of the magazine.

Cynthia is sold on the power of networking. It's not a frivolous endeavor that takes you away from the job. It *is* the job.

CYNTHIA GOOD'S TIPS FOR NETWORKING SUCCESS:

1. Network to help others as well as yourself. All the common sayings—what goes around comes around; the more you give, the more you get; and so on—are really true.

2. Target one key person. Instead of giving out cards to the masses, pinpoint the key figures who can help you accomplish your goals. If you can't get to a certain decision maker immediately, find someone in his or her organization who will support your cause.

3. Make yourself prominent in the community. Join a nonprofit board, make speeches, and write articles and blogs (even for free) as a way to establish yourself as an expert and widen your network.

4. Tap into the virtual world. Social and professional online networks are growing fast and can be a great place to make alliances and keep customers up to date.

5. Close the deal. Now that you know how to build a network, make sure it works for you. Practice asking for what you want!

BIG IDEA TOOLBOX
NETWORKING RESOURCES

* LinkedIn.com (www.linkedin.com): An online network of more than 20 million experienced professionals from around the world, representing 150 industries.

* Zoom Information, Inc. (www.zoominfo.com): An extensive business search engine with profiles on more than thirty-five million people and three million companies.
* BUZGate—Business Utility Zone Gateway (www.buzgate. org): A resource portal for start-ups and small businesses.
* *The Virtual Handshake: Opening Doors and Closing Deals Online*, by David Teten and Scott Allen.

When in Doubt, Throw a Party

I wrote about Richard Kirshenbaum in my first book, *Often Wrong, Never in Doubt*. Richie was the original "Why NOT me?" guy—a creative, ballsy ad man with a shtick a mile long and the talent to back it up. He was the first person I hired at Deutsch, but Richie was setting his sights higher. He left after two years to join J. Walter Thompson, and then almost immediately jumped ship to start his own agency with a JWT coworker. When I heard about the launch of Kirshenbaum Bond & Partners, I laughed it off. I mean, I loved the guy, but he was like twenty-six or twenty-seven at the time. He had no business starting an ad agency. But soon after his start-up, Richie landed the account for Kenneth Cole shoes and launched a daring social message campaign that took the ad world by storm. Suddenly, he was being written up in the press as the advertising flavor of the month. And yeah, I was jealous. That was supposed to be me! But I learned a big lesson from Richie: If you want to be great, you have to put yourself out there and say, "Why NOT me?"

Fast-forward to the present. Richie sits atop a fantastically successful agency, and I have the great pleasure of bringing him on *The Big Idea* as an expert from time to time.

Which brings me to the point about throwing a party. Richie

told a story from the days when his agency was new and trying to get clients. One weekend he picked up a copy of the legendary adman Jerry Della Femina's book, *From Those Wonderful Folks Who Gave You Pearl Harbor*. Della Femina wrote that when he was going *into* business he almost went *out* of business, and as a last resort decided to throw a party. The result: He picked up a few clients and not only stayed in business but became an ad legend. Richie thought it was worth a try. He bartered a party with a restaurant client, and planned a "first annual KBP party."

Richie applied his standard philosophy of nothing-ventured-nothing-gained in making up the guest list. He thought about all the famous and successful people he didn't know and who definitely didn't know him, and he thought, "Why not invite them? Even if they don't come they might remember our name." He also invited reporters and photographers, figuring he might attract them with the free food and drinks.

I was at that party, and I can tell you, it was a real bash, a roaring success. You never would have guessed that Richie had bartered it. He made himself and his agency look successful. And yes, some of the famous and important people did show up—including a couple of future clients.

Richie's advice: "While some may think a party is frivolous or expensive or not worth the energy, my advice, to paraphrase Jerry Della Femina, is *when in doubt, throw a party.* This year we celebrated our twentieth anniversary with our three hundred employees and friends and relatives, and all the people I invited my first year showed up. But I still sent an invitation to Prince Charles and Camilla, because you never know."

DONNY'S DO: IT'S THE PEOPLE, STUPID

The difference between staying small and going big—in *anything* you do in life—is people. I'll go so far as to say, before you start worrying about how you're going to fund your business with money, think about how you're going to build social capital. Money is fickle; social capital just keeps growing, even in hard times.

How do you build social capital when you're just starting out? The mistake many new entrepreneurs make is that they're solely focused on asking others for help. Turn it around. Figure out how you can be the one doing the helping. There's no better first impression you can create than when people see you offering instead of asking.

Breaking Down
the Roadblocks

CHAPTER 18

Dollars and
Sense

Y ou've got a big idea that you know will make millions. You have the passion and drive to make it happen. You've created a mission statement and a solid business plan. You've done your due diligence, studied the market, explored the playing field, and burned up the phone lines making contacts. You've tested your idea with friends and family, attended trade shows, and talked to patent attorneys, manufacturers, and other business owners.

You are at the gate, ready to run, and the bell is about to go off. There is only one thing holding you back: money.

In the previous chapters, you've seen countless examples of people who made millions with only two nickels to rub together—and, yes, that's possible. The very essence of the American dream is that it is available to everyone. That's the message I've preached in this book, and the true inspirational stories of people just like you back that up. But naïvete isn't necessarily a virtue when it comes to matters of cold, hard cash.

The first rule is that you have to put your money where your mouth is. And if you don't have money? Then put your time, energy, and passion where your mouth is. The point is, you've got to give your all to get something back.

How Much Do You Want It?

I have never heard a truly successful entrepreneur say, "It was a breeze. I did it with one hand tied behind my back." We tend to focus on the mountaintop, and applaud those who made it—but we shouldn't let the dazzle of their achievements blind us to the grit, sacrifice and hard work it took to make it happen.

Here's the key question: Do you want it enough to turn your life upside down, live on the cheap, sacrifice comfort, and work your butt off? Do you have the energy, passion, and ability to work 24/7, if that's what it takes? Can you see yourself making one hundred phone calls to get to a yes?

Think about it:

+ *Are there sacrifices you won't consider—such as moving back home with your parents, taking public transportation, driving an economy car, foregoing vacations and dinners out?*
+ *Do you have a high, medium, or low percentage of fixed expenses that tie you down to your current lifestyle?*
+ *Are you willing to dip into savings, home equity, or other resources to fund your business?*
+ *What constitutes an intolerable risk for you?*
+ *Are you willing to start over from a lesser position if your plan fails?*

Your answers to these questions will determine your emotional readiness to pursue your personal American dream.

THE BIG IDEA EXPERTS
MONEY MASTERY

MORE WITH LESS:

"Each time you have money coming in, take 20 percent (or any manageable percentage) and put it into an escrow account. Use the remaining 80 percent to run your business and you will be amazed by how you can adjust." Mike Michalowicz, Obsidian Launch.

STRIKE WHILE THE IRON IS HOT:

"The best time to apply for financing is when you do not need it. If your business is showing a profit and you can get by without taking out a loan, take out a loan anyway. You are far more likely to be approved by a bank if your business is making money, and a line of credit usually won't cost you a penny if you do not draw from it." Paul Lewis, angel investor.

SAVE IT:

"Everything is more expensive than you estimated the first time, and there are always hidden costs. Whatever you estimate the cost of setting up the business to be, you should set aside as much as 25–50 percent more, just in case." Jerry Lynch, financial adviser with JFL Innovative Investments.

The Best Money a Big Idea Can Buy

What would it take for you to be able to say "Money is not an obstacle"? Here are six ways to fund your business:

1. Use Your Own Money.

There's no better sign of commitment than a willingness to put your own resources on the line. It's also a way of maintaining control. If you're investing in yourself, that tells others you have the confidence and the self-motivation to get your idea to market. And if you do eventually seek support from others, they'll want to know that you opened your own bank account first. Go ahead—max the credit cards, tap your savings, unload the second car, sell great-grandmother's diamond ring, refinance your mortgage, skip the vacation, move back in with Dad and Mom. Don't be stupid about it—you still have to pay taxes and steer clear of the collection agencies. But this is a true test of how much you want it.

2. Borrow from Family and Friends.

Laura Rowley, a *Big Idea* expert, financial consultant, and author, offers the following tips for approaching family and friends: Time and again, family and friends are the best source of funding for new businesses. But you have to keep it on the up-and-up. This is not a favor; it's hopefully an opportunity for everyone to prosper. Approach family and friends as you would any other investors, with a full accounting of your business plan and expectations—including the best- and worst- case scenarios. Be sure to consult a financial adviser and write up a formal contract. Use a lending network designed for interfamily loans, such as CircleLending.com. Tools at that site will help you and your relatives come to terms on the length of the loan and the interest rate, and calculate the monthly payment amount. For ninety-nine dollars, CircleLending issues a legally binding promissory note and a repayment schedule.

And one caveat—know your loved ones. If you think a business transaction has the potential to create friction, look elsewhere. It's just not worth it.

3. Check Out Peer-to-Peer Lending.

As Laura Rowley notes, "Several Web sites now make it much easier to find an investor who will back your business. Check out Prosper.com, Lending club.com and Zopa.com. Lending Club, which launched on Face book in May 2007 and later on its own site, uses technology to match borrowers to lenders willing to offer unsecured loans of $500 to $25,000 with three-year, fully amortizing terms. The distinctive angle here: The search technology looks for social connections between the borrower and the lender—maybe you went to the same college, or worked at the same company in the past. Potential borrowers are weighed on the same criteria a bank would use—a FICO score of at least 640 and a debt-to-income ratio of 25 percent or less, excluding mortgages. Late payments are reported to credit bureaus.

"Prosper.com is the largest person-to-person lender, with 430,000 members lending $91 million to one another in the first year. The borrower profiles are extensive, including the repayment history of other Prosper loans and endorsements from friends who have bid on the loan."

4. Apply for a Small Business Loan.

Don't forget the government. "The U.S. Small Business Administration makes loans through local banks and agencies; you can use these loans to buy equipment, inventory, furniture, supplies, and more," suggests Laura Rowley. Within the agency, there are a variety of special loan programs for women and minorities. There are also other special business loan programs, designed for people who have special needs. An example is the Self Employment Loan Fund, which gives small loans and training to low-income entrepreneurs.

Another great resource is Count Me In, the leading not-for-profit provider of micro loans and business resources for women entrepreneurs. Apply to the Make Mine a Million $ Business awards program to get the assistance to grow your micro business to a million-dollar enterprise. It's amazing how a small financial boost can be a major launching pad.

5. Partner Up.

Big Idea expert Mike Michalowicz, of Obsidian Launch, suggests, "Contact vendors and tell them your vision, goals, and financial needs. They will have a good understanding of your market and a really good understanding of you. As your business grows, with their help, your needs for their services will increase, too. A win-win situation all around."

Remember Jim Koch of Sam Adams beer? His decision to partner up with a small brewery allowed him to get started—and you can bet the brewery thanked its lucky stars a million times over the years.

6. Find an Angel.

As Laura Rowley points out, "This is where to turn when you have gone through your own funds and exhausted investment possibilities with family and friends. Angel investors are high net worth investors who are willing to invest their own money in your business. Start with the Angel Capital Education Foundation, which has a listing of angel groups. The typical range of financing is between \$100,000 and \$500,000 in exchange for a fairly large chunk of your equity."

Our *Big Idea* expert, angel investor Paul Lewis, notes, "Since most angels provide equity financing, there is usually no need to pay the money back. Of course, different investors have different rules, so it is important to clearly understand the terms of the agreement. If your company is losing money, make sure you

BIG IDEA TOOLBOX
RESOURCES FOR FUNDING

FINANCIAL COACHING

* The Money Coach (www.themoneycoach.com): A step-by-step guide to growing your wealth.
* MoneyandHappiness.com (www.moneyandhappiness. com): Laura Rowley's business and finance advice—with the right attitude.
* *Money and Happiness: A Guide to Living the Good Life*, by Laura Rowley.

FAMILY LENDING

* Circle Lending (www.circlelending.com): Information and practical support for family lending.

PEER-TO-PEER LENDING

* LendingClub.com (www.lendingclub.com): A personal loan and lending investment company.
* Prosper.com (www.prosper.com): Personal peer lending, up to \$2,500.
* Zopa.com (www.zopa.com): A site for lenders and borrowers.

(continued)

LOANS

* Small Business Administration (www.sba.gov): The government's full-service department for helping small businesses, including a variety of special loan programs.
* Count Me In (www.countmein.org): Resources for women entrepreneurs.

ANGEL INVESTORS

* The Angel Capital Education Foundation (www.angel capitaleducation.org): A charitable organization for research and information in the field of angel investing.
* The Angel Capital Association (www.angelcapital association.org): A professional alliance of angel groups.

VENTURE CAPITAL

* Topspin partners (www.topspinpartners.com): A venture capital firm.
* National Venture Capital Association (www.nvca.org): An information and support tool for businesses seeking venture capital.
* Springboard Enterprises (www.springboardenterprises .org): A national non-profit organization that accelerates women's access to equity markets.

understand why before speaking to an angel. An angel will not be interested in financing your business if he or she thinks it is just a hobby for you. If you have tapped out all of your credit cards, cannot get another dime from your parents, and are too small to be noticed by a venture capitalist, an angel may be your perfect solution."

DONNY'S DO: GET IT FOR NOTHING

A successful business brings in more money than it puts out. So, while you're working on the first part, figure out how you can spend less. Alan Corey, the author of *A Million Bucks by 30*, shared some ingenious cost-cutting ideas with *The Big Idea*. My favorites—never buy an umbrella; it's a rain tax. Never buy bottled water; you're paying for a container. The point is, look around and see where you're pissing away the bucks, and stop doing it. The same applies to starting a business. What can you get for nothing—or next to nothing?

Research: It doesn't cost anything to think and dream. It's also free to brainstorm with friends, wander the mall, and browse the Internet. There is a wealth of information for start-ups that's a click away.

Office space: The virtual office is the new frontier. You can start your business on your dining room table and make the same impact as someone sitting in the corner office of a skyscraper.

Publicity: We talked about this. Make news and get noticed for free.

Expert advice: Browse some of the Web sites we've recommended in this book. You'll be amazed at how much you can learn without spending a cent. And don't forget to watch *The Big Idea* and visit our Web site. We give it away for nothing every day.

CHAPTER 19

Perfect
Pitch

'll admit it. There's a special place in my heart for people who blow the lid off with an outlandish pitch. They do something unexpected and outrageous to make their case. They're willing to risk rejection and ridicule, and even be a little irritating on the hunch that it just might work.

My first big client pitch, when I was just starting to grow my dad's agency, falls in the category of sheer insanity. By a stroke of luck, we'd been given a chance to pitch the Pontiac Dealers Association, which represented one hundred dealers in the New York–New Jersey–Connecticut tri-state area. That was the good news. The bad news was that we'd be competing with twenty other agencies, and we had *nada*. No television experience, no auto experience—nothing obvious that would make us the natural choice. What we did have was hunger, an undying belief that we could do it, and the guts to give an outrageous pitch.

The guy making the hiring decision was an old advertising pro named Bob Conroy. He'd seen it all, as they say. But we were ballsy enough to think we could give Bob something he hadn't seen before. We went to a junkyard and collected a bunch of old auto parts. Every half hour for twelve hours, we delivered a different part to Bob's house in Westport, Connecticut. A headlight, with a tag that read: "We'll give you bright ideas." A fender, with a tag that read: "We'll protect your rear end." A steering wheel, with a tag that read: "We'll steer you in the right direction." By the end of the day, we'd delivered an entire car—and our message.

It could have backfired. Who wants a driveway full of car parts in a high-class neighborhood like Westport? But Bob got it—and loved it. He invited us to be one of five agencies to pitch the account, and we ended up landing the deal.

I learned something from that experience that I've never forgotten. Guys like Bob Conroy exist in every business. You've just got to find your Bob Conroy—the person who will respond.

I still love an outrageous pitch. My all-time favorite, on *The Big Idea*, came from BlendTec. Tom Dickson invented a new blender, which you'd think would be kind of a ho hum enterprise—like inventing a new coffee cup. But Tom's "Will It Blend?" campaign turned it into a forty-million-dollar business, and made him a cult hero on YouTube. Tom's idea was to showcase his blender's remarkable capability by putting it to the test with household stuff that no one in his right mind would ever put in a blender—iPods, TV remotes, golf balls, hearing aids, toys, credit cards, and DVDs. People tuned in to see what he would blend next. When he blended an iPhone, the powder sold for nine hundred dollars on eBay. Tom's wacky idea was a hit, and the bottom line proves it.

Big Idea Lesson: You can market a rock if it's fresh and funny. In fact, someone did! A guy named Gary Dahl made millions in the 1970s with the Pet Rock.

The Art of Self-Branding

Deion Sanders is a master of self-promotion. He was also a hell of a defensive back, and a pretty decent baseball player. He is the only player to have appeared in both the Super Bowl (for the 49ers and Cowboys) and the World Series (for the Braves). He always stood out on the field—famous for his do-rag and his "high stepping" when he scored a touchdown. You couldn't miss this guy, but Deion wasn't just an empty jersey. From the time he was a kid, he had an insatiable appetite to be the best, and he worked and studied his butt off to get there. He knew he was good and wasn't afraid to say so. "I'm the best thing since peanut butter and jelly," he used to tell his mom. But Deion's most important observation, when he came on *The Big Idea*, was, "When the bright light shines, it also shows your blemishes, so you've got to have the goods."

I relate to the guy. In the past, I've been criticized for being a self-promoter. They have words for people like me, and they don't sound so flattering—arrogant, cocky, bad boy—you've heard them all. But say what they will, I'm successful not because I'm cocky, but because I always made sure I had the goods.

Self-promotion is not about arrogance. It's about branding. I created my brand as a brash, upstart, creative ad guy. That brand enabled Deutsch to get our agency on the playing field. Everyone knew we were fearless. So, if you have a product or service to pitch, you have to start with that essential question— what's the Joe or Jennifer or Sarah brand? It requires you to dig deeper than the immediate appeal of your product and service.

Ty Pennington is another example of someone who has created a brand out of himself. I like the guy because he was another one of those ADD kids who never fit in. He once said he used to strip down naked and swing from the blinds in his classroom as a child. God love him. (Today he's a spokesperson for the organization ADHD Experts on Call.)

Ty was a set designer for television and movies when he was tapped for a new show called *Trading Spaces*. That's where he really shined. Viewers loved Ty's zany, irreverent humor, but they also came to trust his great design sense. He went on lead the team on *Extreme Makeover: Home Edition*, which led to a deal with Sears for the Ty Pennington Style line of bedding, tabletop items, bath accessories, and other miscellaneous home decor. When people buy his products, they're buying into Ty's style and dream. He's a brand!

> **Big Idea Lesson: Define your brand—that unique appeal that only you can create.**

Winning Hearts and Minds

At Deutsch we had a philosophy that our ads were never designed merely to sell a product. They were designed to win the hearts and minds of the audience. We were wholly focused on the underlying human quest, the core value—what the product represented for the customer. Think about it. Why does one person buy Glacéau water while another person swears by Fiji? What statement is someone making by drinking SmartWater or VitaminWater? You can talk all you want about how one is purer or healthier or tastes better, but the biggest difference among all the different waters on the market is their emotional appeal, and the way they uniquely cater to the desire to be sexy or cool or health-conscious. If you understand your market's values, you'll be able to devise a perfect pitch.

Starbucks is a superior example of this. Howard Schultz, who conceived the idea, understood that people were looking for a community, a living room experience—the kind they'd have around a cup of coffee. He didn't pitch the coffee, he pitched the social longing.

But here's an important caveat. There is a tangible benefit and an emotional benefit, and you have to be able to fulfill both. In advertising lingo, this is called "the bar defense"—because liquor is the perfect example. If you line up twenty bottles of vodka on the bar, your customers are going to choose the one that fits their self-image. But no one is going to say, "I drink Grey Goose because it makes me look hot." You also have to give them a bar defense—the tangible benefits of one vodka over another. Customers need a rational explanation for why they do emotionally driven things.

Take It Away!

Do your palms sweat at the very idea of picking up the phone to make that call? Well, join the club. Everyone, no matter how big they are, is nervous at the moment before a pitch. I can remember going into the bathroom and talking to the mirror before a big pitch, trying to pump myself up. Like most things, it's a head trip. So, here's what you do to get past it.

1. Find the human connection. Whether you're pitching a buyer, a manufacturer, an investor, or the media, remember that you're talking to a real person. Companies don't make decisions. People make decisions. When you're face-to-face with a decision maker, engage that person where they live. It used to be a standard suggestion for nervous performers that they imagine their audience naked. That's not what I'm talking about. Your task is not to diminish your target so you'll feel superior, it's to connect by establishing a common bond.

2. Pick the right person. You wouldn't pitch a buyer for Neiman Marcus on discount sportswear. The last thing you want is the "doesn't fit our needs" speech before you've even got a foot in the door. Do your homework and be able to articulate clearly and succinctly how your product or service meets the needs of the audience that person represents.

3. Rehearse until you have it down flat. Brainstorm every possible question you might be asked, and have a clear and succinct answer. Be very specific about what you want this person to do for you.

4. Show your passion. The first thing I look for when I listen to a pitch is whether a person has the fire to see it through. I want to know that he or she has what it takes to make sacrifices and overcome obstacles over the long haul. The best idea in the world will fall flat if it isn't backed up by passion. Show that you're willing to do the heavy lifting and are not just looking for a free ride.

5. Be respectful. Your prospect has agreed to give you five or ten minutes of precious time. Watch the arrogance. Don't go in with an attitude of "This is your lucky day." Instead, listen and respond respectfully. Actually, one of the most respectful things you can do is to adhere to tip number three—be prepared. And after the meeting? This seems obvious—didn't your mother always tell you to write thank-you notes? But a surprising number of people don't take the natural, gracious, and productive step of saying thank you. A pitch isn't over when you walk out the door.

KNOCKING ON HEAVEN'S DOOR
AMILYA ANTONETTI ON GETTING
PAST THE SWITCHBOARD

What you need is a champion within your target company to help you get a meeting with the decision makers. Therefore, you need to create a win/win for a marketing director, sales manager, or maybe even a vendor that does business with your target business to help facilitate this meeting. Consider how you, as a business owner, like to be approached to hear new information and/or ideas. What would cause you to pause and ask to hear more? This is a great time to put on your creative hat and think of things that you can do to help someone else's agenda inside the organization. Everyone is trying to get something done, reach someone, or build a relationship. Every time I have helped someone get what they need, I was then able to have an attentive ear on what I was proposing.

Read more of Amilya's advice on The Big Idea *Web site (www .cnbc.com).*

The Elevator Pitch

I believe there are about three meetings in a person's career that have the potential to change their life forever. The elevator pitch is one of them.

The idea of an elevator pitch is simple: If you found yourself in an elevator with a big investor, how would you pitch him or her in the time it takes to get from the lobby to the investor's floor? The game time is very narrow—maybe ninety seconds.

Here's the signature of an elevator pitch. You've got a tight amount of time, and you've got to close the deal. You've got to be fast, passionate, get to the point, and get the job done.

It's a real challenge and a real opportunity. We developed our Elevator Pitch segment on *The Big Idea* to give entrepreneurs looking for an angel investor their chance of a lifetime.

The first time we taped the Elevator Pitch show, the atmosphere was electric and tense. We used a real elevator at 30 Rock, the home of NBC, in the heart of Manhattan. Our angel investor was Paul Lewis, a guy who has built four multimillion-dollar companies from the ground floor and now invests in people's dreams.

Our entrepreneur was Monica Williams, a young doctor turned businesswoman who created a product she believed would make millions. Pacimals is a detachable pacifier connected to a stuffed toy, making it easier for young babies to hold. A very simple, beautifully executed product. Monica had 80,000 orders and needed investment money to start getting them shipped and grow her business. She'd be asking Paul for an investment of $250,000. In return, Paul would ask her some tough questions: What were the benefits of the product? What would additional capital do? What was the growth potential of the business?

Monica had a lot riding on her elevator ride. Angel investors like Paul hear pitches all the time, so in her ninety-second window of opportunity she had to get his attention, rock his world, perk up his ears. Paul's rule for a perfect pitch? "Be brief, be bright, be gone." I love it.

Monica's elevator ride with Paul could produce one of three results. Paul could say, "I'm interested. Come into my office and let's talk more." He could say, "I may be interested in the future, once you do x, y, or z." Or he could say, "Sorry, I'm not interested."

It was high suspense for all of us because we didn't know the ending. But when Paul and Monica came out of the elevator, we saw she'd scored a hit. As the father of four, Paul recognized Monica's product as something he would have liked to have when his kids were young. She got him with the personal touch, and followed up with a strong presentation.

The Elevator Pitch isn't like a game show where the contestant walks away with a big check. Paul's interest was only the first step in the negotiating process. But Monica was on her way.

The Elevator Pitch has been a wildly popular segment on *The Big Idea*, because of the sheer potential to watch dreams come true. But we're also trying to provide a training ground for every entrepreneur. Here's some practical advice from the investor's mouth.

PAUL LEWIS'S DO'S AND DON'TS FOR PITCHING AN INVESTOR:

DO: Be prepared. The investor is interviewing you, and if you do not know the answers the game is over. Know everything you can about your product, the competition, the opportunity, and the market.

DO: Know exactly how much money you need and exactly what you are going to use it for. Talk in specifics. If you need $248,573, say so. Do not talk in ranges.

DO: Know exactly what you're willing to give up in exchange for the investment, whether it is equity or an interest rate. Know your terms and make them clear.

DO: Be 100 percent honest. If you are having difficulties, say so. If you just lost a big account, say so. The investor will learn the facts before making an investment, so don't waste his time or your time.

DON'T: Lie. If you lie, it's the kiss of death. Game over. Period.

DON'T: Be desperate. Show the investor that you have confidence in your product.

DON'T: Ask the investor how much he wants to invest. Instead, tell him what you need. It is perfectly fine to ask if your needs are within his range, but stick to specifics.

DON'T: Paint a rosy picture. Being optimistic is fine, but don't oversell the business or the concept. If the deal is meant to be, it will happen.

QVC: The Big Pitch

Every entrepreneur dreams of making the ultimate pitch—to the audience of QVC. The enormity of QVC's influence is hard to fathom. The twenty-four-hour-a-day broadcast introduces more than 1,600 products every week—many of them brand-new items never seen before. QVC can turn an unknown into a household name in twenty minutes. It's a ticket to opportunity, wholly dependent on your ability to sell America on your big idea.

One of our favorite guests was a QVC success story named Kim Babjak. Before she had her big idea, the potential of this ninth-grade dropout who served up French fries for ten dollars an hour at McDonald's was hidden from everyone, including herself. Kim was like millions of people—a hardworking wife and mother living near the bottom rung of the economy. One day Kim was struggling to hoist her king-sized mattress so she could remove the bedskirt, and it just wouldn't budge. She ended up calling upon three of her neighbors to help, and that's what fueled her idea. Realizing that she couldn't enlist an army of help every time she needed to perform this practical household task, Kim began to tinker with a solution. She sewed a zipper the length of a bedskirt and created a prototype for Zip-a-Ruffle, the first detachable bedskirt.

Big Idea Lesson: QVC is in the business of finding new products to bring to market. They cannot exist without you. That understanding will empower you to say, "Why not *my* product?"

Kim didn't know anything about launching a product, so she went to the local chapter of Retired Service Corps of America and got invaluable advice from the expert counselors. Then Kim registered for the Self Employment Loan Fund's ten-week workshop on writing a business plan. Upon graduation, Kim launched her product with a thousand-dollar SELF loan, and began to achieve small local success. But three years in, she decided to go for broke and take on the biggest challenge of all—getting her product on QVC. She hired a QVC agent to help her, and it paid off. After her QVC success, Wal-Mart approached her about selling Zip-a-Ruffle in its stores. What a great position to be in! Her success gave Kim the confidence to expand her business to other products, and now she's the one giving advice to start-up businesses. In fact, Kim is a QVC agent herself!

DONNY'S DO: NOTHING IS SACRED

Just when you think you've seen it all, someone steps up with a mind blower. This is a true story. One day, taping a live show, I spent some time chatting with the audience. When I opened the floor for questions, a very conventional-looking, middle-aged woman came to the microphone to ask about her big idea. What was it? An inflatable condom! At first, I thought it was a gag, but she was absolutely serious as she primly described the benefits for men with small equipment. "Can I say penis?" she asked shyly. The audience roared. Well, never say never. But I did voice one practical concern. "You might have trouble identifying your target audience," I told her.

CHAPTER 20

Make Trade Show
Magic

The trade show is the epicenter of entrepreneurial activity. A trade show can be the best investment of time and money you will ever make. It's where new ideas take root and blossom. Virtually every industry has trade shows, and they can allow new entrepreneurs to showcase their stuff for relatively little money.

I've met many entrepreneurs who had their biggest breaks at trade shows. But the value of a trade show goes far beyond actual deal making. It's also a great arena for networking and learning. You may be the small fish in the big pond, but even a small fish can swim around, observe, and make an impact.

BIG IDEA TOOLBOX
TACKLING THE TRADE SHOW

* **Trade Show Exhibitors Association** (www.tsea.org): Provides a comprehensive array of trade show resources and information to sales, marketing, and management

(continued)

professionals who use trade shows and events to promote their products and services.

* **International Association of Exhibitions and Events** (www.iaee.org): Represents the interests of more than 3,500 trade show and exposition managers globally.

* **Corporate Event Marketing Association** (www.cemaonline .com): A nonprofit organization dedicated to serving event and marketing professionals in all sectors of the technology industry by providing educational and networking opportunities.

* **Comprehensive Trade Show Vendor Resource** (www .trade-show-vendors.com): An online trade show guide offering hundreds of hand-picked trade show resources for successful events, business meetings, and conferences. The guide includes sources for event promotion, booth attractions, convention planning services, giveaways, booth design, lodging, transportation, and more.

* **The Trade Show News Network** (www.tsnn.com): Publications devoted to trade show news and ideas.

* *Tradeshow Week* (www.tradeshowweek.com): The magazine of the trade show industry.

The Road to CES

How do you get your big idea in front of the people who can help you take it to the next step? On *The Big Idea* we decided to jump in with both feet and find out if we could make trade show magic happen for a group of start-ups.

We chose the Consumer Electronics Show (CES) as our launching pad. CES is the largest international electronics trade show in the world. CES has been making magic for over forty years, introducing products that have become household necessities—such as the camcorder, Nintendo, the VCR, the DVD player, and HDTV. CES presents an unrivaled opportunity, but also a huge challenge for someone just trying to get off the ground. With almost three thousand exhibitors and one hundred and fifty thousand attendees, how do you stand out and make your mark?

"The Road to CES" chronicled four budding entrepreneurs from pre-game to post-game, using our team of experts to take them through the steps.

Each of our entrepreneurs had demonstrated three essential qualities:

1. **An innovative technology.**
2. **Market worthiness.**
3. **Passion to succeed at all costs.**

I think these new tech developers are the most interesting people. They're not only going through all the regular steps any new business faces. They're dealing in true futures. In the tech world, you have to have it in your blood—in addition to having a unique skill set. It's a very different deal from the entrepreneur who says, "There's a hole in the clothing market. I'm going to introduce a new pair of jeans." The tech wiz starts with more. So right off the bat, I'm a little in awe of this gang.

Having said that, the dynamics of "The Road to CES" were universal. These four companies had the same goals of any new business trying to crack a market. With thousands of people walking around, what can you do to grab their attention and say, "Look at me"? Well, obviously, *The Big Idea* gave them a leg up in that arena, but the point is, they had to sell it or it wasn't going to happen.

Let's look at our four entrepreneurs and their show highlights.

LIGHTGLOVE: A HANDS-FREE INFRARED COMPUTER CONTROLLER

When Bruce Howard's mother developed carpal tunnel syndrome, Bruce, who worked in optics, decided to develop a lightglove that could control a cursor by infrared light, without having to touch the keyboard. Since then, he extended the utility of the product, which has special potential in the gaming industry.

Lightglove is a revolutionary product, which Bruce and his wife, M.G., have spent years developing. This couple has passion, and Bruce has the genius to make it work. Right off the bat, they had a victory at CES when Lightglove was awarded the CES Best of Innovations Award for Electronic Gaming, beating out billion-dollar companies such as Dell and Logitech. They also suffered a disappointment when our angel investor, Paul Lewis, declined to invest in their product. Paul felt they weren't ready—and a big reason was that they didn't have a winning pitch. They hadn't worked out the numbers. Our experts felt that their next step was to sit down with a business consultant, and work out the nuts and bolts of exactly how they were going to take their great idea to market.

Big Idea Lesson: Don't romanticize your product at the expense of developing a business. Investors are going to want to know that you're ready to roll it out, and that they can have confidence in your business acumen. If you can't do it, hire those who can.

BUG LABS: A MODULAR, WIRELESS GPS DEVICE

After 9/11, Pete Semmelhack thought about how traumatic it was for people to be unable to reach their loved ones. He designed a modular wireless personal GPS device that would take the worry out of separation.

Bug Labs went into CES with a clear advantage and a clear

disadvantage. The advantage was that it was an extreme techie product, and this was a techie crowd. The disadvantage was that it was a niche product—by a geek for geeks.

Our experts all had a problem with the name Bug Labs, which they didn't think was edgy enough. But Peter did something very right at CES—he worked the blogger community. Bloggers are the most committed geeks; they're able to spread the word faster than Peter could ever have managed on his own with more traditional PR. Bloggers are the new inroad—there was even a Blog Bus at the show.

> **Big Idea Lesson: If you're a geek, talk to the geeks. Find your niche and don't be distracted by the big box stores.**

MOGO: AN ALL-IN-ONE WIRELESS MOUSE

Matt Westover saw the future and it was mobile. He recognized a need for wireless peripherals that you could take on the road, but the only devices currently available were made for desktops. He created a sleek, flat mouse that could go anywhere—and went up against the most established computer companies.

Matt's product is sexy and smart. The timing for it is perfect, as laptop sales are getting ready to outsell desktops for the first time ever.

Matt's big challenge at the show was to create buzz, because his product already hit the mark. Matt really threw himself into CES, and he had the right spirit for the Vegas setting. He made a big hit with the MoGo GoGo Girls, who wore MoGo branded tops, carried MoGos, and struck up conversations to demonstrate the product. Then they offered each listener a twenty-dollar discount coupon. The MoGo GoGo girls made a splash at CES,

> **Big Idea Lesson: Even a small company can make a big impact. Matt found a way to gain access to show attendees, working outside the booth.**

and they distributed thousands of discount coupons, which will potentially turn into sales.

H2O AUDIO: A WATERPROOF MP3 CASE AND EARPHONES

Kristian Rauhala's passion for water sports led to his invention. He wanted to be able to listen to music while surfing, scuba diving, and swimming. His product has all the marks of a winner. Radio Shack thought so, too. Kristian scored the big "get" of CES, when Radio Shack began negotiations to sell his product in its stores.

H2O Audio is an interesting case. We all loved Kristian's passion for surfing, and his device was beautifully crafted. But with Radio Shack knocking at the door, Kristian needed to expand his vision—fast. Radio Shack customers encompass a broad market—not just diehard surfers. To be successful, Kristian needed

Big Idea Lesson: Always be ready to expand your vision and find new applications for your product that will attract new customers.

to widen his target to reach beyond water sports enthusiasts to bathtub dreamers and shower singers.

Each of our four companies came away from CES with something enormously valuable. Seeing them go through the process in real time was a great experience for all of us, and for our viewers.

STAND UP AND STAND OUT

Nicole Hait, with INPEX, the largest trade show for inventors, offers these four tips for making an impact at a trade show.

1. **Have an eye-catching display.** When you're competing in a huge arena, sitting side by side with gigantic multimillion-dollar displays, it's a challenge to stand out. But you don't have to spend a fortune to be noticed. You can't compete with the big guys on being lavish, so figure out a way to be different.
2. **Create a gimmick or giveaway to get people to your booth.** People love free stuff. It doesn't have to be big. Give away a pen, a stress ball, pretzels. Hold a raffle. It will be money well spent.
3. **Be energetic.** Don't sit in your booth with your feet up, eating a sandwich or reading the newspaper. Stay "on."
4. **Have your pitch ready.** Memorize it—you may have only a few seconds to state your case.

Rules of the Road

How do you make trade show magic? Follow these simple rules, courtesy of Mike Michalowicz. Mike, one of our *Big Idea* experts, is the founder of Obsidian Launch, a business growth accelerator that partners exclusively with young, first-time entrepreneurs. Mike has a driving passion for entrepreneurialism. It is his belief that anyone with the desire—even a fleeting "what if"—has been touched by an inspiration that must be satisfied. Mike's wisdom is invaluable for first and even second time trade show attendees.

GOING IN . . .

✦ *Preparation is a must. Many know this, but only a few act on it. Find out who is going to be there ahead of time and determine who you want to meet and where you can find them.*

✦ *Give a heads-up. Weeks before the show, reach out to the people you want to meet and arrange a time to get together at the show. Don't leave the key networking opportunities to chance.*

✦ *Give them the materials in advance. There will be so much going on at the show, your stuff will probably go into the big bag of garbage literature. Send your materials and literature to key individuals ahead of time. Follow it up with a meeting at the show.*

AT THE SHOW...

✦ *Run a spread offense. The key here is teaming up and spreading out. Have a couple of people manning your booth, and a couple of people walking the floor.*

✦ *This is go time. Go and network. In addition to your prearranged meetings, do a lot of rapid networking. Not card pushing, but networking. If you meet people who you can help or who can help you, get their cards and tell them you will follow up the week after the show.*

✦ *Stand out. You've got to be different if you want to draw traffic. But different doesn't always mean outrageous. Find simple ways to make your booth worth a second look.*

✦ *Use the 80/20 Rule. Generally, 80 percent of the traffic coming to your booth is of no value, and only 20 percent are real opportunities. To make matters worse, another 80 percent of the qualified opportunities don't even know you have a booth at the show. Put the odds in your favor by notifying key attendees in advance and by having a booth that is unique to their needs.*

THE AFTER-PARTY...

✦ *You've just begun. Successful trade show events are followed up with consistent and persistent contact. During the show you should have identified key contacts, and now is the time to do the follow-up.*

✦ *It's not just the next day, it's the next year. Just like a bell curve, all the activity surrounding a trade show dies off a few days after the event. Prepare to keep your follow-up campaign going for the long haul.*

✦ *It's just around the corner. The next show is only a year away. Keep your key contacts apprised of what you're doing, and make plans to see them again at next year's event.*

DONNY'S DO: COMPETITION, *WHAT* COMPETITION?

We live in a free market, and that's a great thing. It means the door is wide open. But a lot of new businesses are paralyzed by their fear of the competition. They worry that someone else is going to muscle in on their territory, knock off their great product and sell it for less, or cost them a fortune fighting for control.

I find that the best entrepreneurs are *not* obsessed with the competition. They can't wait to get their ideas out in the world. It's the nature of business that if you have a great new idea, chances are someone else will be nipping at your heels. Ilana Diamond, president of Sima Products, who knows a thing or two about cutthroat competition, points out that knock-offs are a fact of life these days. "As fast as your company can create successful products, competitors can begin copying them just as quickly, sometimes within months or even weeks," she points out. Ilana says that the best way to combat knock-offs is to stay ahead of them. Keep close to your customers, and find out what they like and don't like about your products. Improve constantly. Be first. Compete with your own products, before the competition can.

This is terrific advice. Spend your time and resources on your own innovation and development, not on the competition. And when you do think about the competition, use it as a guide that will push you further. Always focus on the US, not on the THEM.

CHAPTER 21

The Hungry
Millionaire

Congratulations—you've made it to your first million. Now what? You should be proud to have reached such an important milestone, but this is no time for complacency. What are you going to do to stay on top of your game—and keep growing?

The business landscape is littered with the corpses of companies that nosedived after early successes. I'm always impressed when I see a company that has avoided this fate—a company like the Container Store. Since its humble beginnings with an investment of only $35,000, the Container Store has become a regular destination for millions of shoppers. It's a huge business, but the founders, Kip Tindell and Garrett Boone, achieved this by never resting on their success. They rely on a set of fundamental business values centered on "creative merchandising, superior customer service, and constant employee input." The Container Store is a perfect business model for any company that wants to stay fresh and relevant while it grows.

The most successful people I know have the ability to maintain an almost naïve sense of wonder even as they accumulate age and experience. They challenge the normal expectation—which is that as you get older and more seasoned, you become more conservative and risk-averse.

Millionaires must stay hungry. Ask any business superstar, and he or she will tell you that the day your stomach feels full is the beginning of the end of your climb. Once that quality that drove your success—hunger—is satisfied, you've lost your most important business tool.

I talked earlier about how this happened to me when I was at Deutsch. I could feel it in my bones—I just wasn't hungry anymore. It had all become too routine. I didn't want to get on a plane at 8:00 in the morning, fly to San Francisco, drive two hours to Modesto, sit for two hours in front of the Gallos making my pitch, drive two hours back, and take a red-eye home. Ugh. I'd lost the hunger. That's when I knew it was time to move on.

It may not happen the same way for you, but watch for the signs that your belly is full, and act quickly. Change direction. Add a product. Take your company in a different direction. Gnaw on a few new bones. Never be satisfied.

The Competitive Edge

If you want your company to be strong and last long, there's no better business mentor than David Novak, CEO of Yum! brands. David is at the top, but his personality and attitude embody all the phases of his life: his childhood spent in thirty-two trailer parks in twenty-three states, his lowly stint as a $7,200-a-year ad copywriter, his many corporate jobs, and his current position running the world's largest restaurant business (including KFC, Taco Bell, Pizza Hut, Long John Silver, and A&W All-American Food), which employs almost one million people. You can literally see the trailer park kid and the striver in his eyes. He hasn't lost it. And that consistency of identity and values has been the key to greatness.

David joined us on *The Big Idea* to share his wisdom—and I promise you, these gems of advice have the potential to make a major difference in your life and business, if you take them to heart:

✦ *Be right-sized. Don't look up, don't look down—always look straight ahead. Be humble. Treat the CEO exactly the same as the guy running the elevator.*
✦ *Avoid stereotypes. David told us how much he hated it when he was young and people made negative assumptions about him because he lived in a trailer park. He vowed that he would never do that to others. As a result, he has been able to recognize genius where some people wouldn't look for it.*
✦ *Create a culture of reward and recognition. It doesn't matter whether you're dealing with a highly ranked executive or someone who's taking orders in a restaurant, you can never underestimate the power of telling someone they're doing a good job.*

There's nothing fancy about these concepts. You won't necessarily learn them at business school, and, in fact, David never went to business school. But these principles have the potential to give every business a competitive edge.

Growing, Growing, Gone!

Let's step back for a moment for a reality check. You've launched your business, you're rolling along, growing and piling up the orders. The marketplace is clamoring for your product. What could go wrong?

One pitfall that can face businesses when they start to turbo to the next level is the temptation to take shortcuts. It's understandable. Last year you were selling five hundred widgets. This year you have orders for twenty thousand, and the demand to produce and supply can be crushing. Your bottom line may be healthy, but suddenly you start dreaming about an even greater profit margin. Here's a cautionary tale for every business that's in danger of getting too big for its britches.

Stacey Blume grew up surrounded by industrial emblems in her father's uniform company. While most people wouldn't consider a bus driver's uniform to be a likely inspiration for a fashion line, Stacey envisioned stylish lingerie and contemporary couture with personalized patches that women would love. After hand sewing some items and selling them at trunk shows, she knew she'd hit on a big idea. Blume Girl Underwear was launched in 2003, and her company made headlines when Jennifer Lopez celebrated her engagement to Ben Affleck by getting a "Ben" patch on her thong underwear. The timing was perfect. Since it was the height of the "Bennifer" phenomenon, *People* magazine and the *Today* show were happy to report the sexy scoop.

Blume was up and running, and the orders were piling in faster than the seamstresses could sew. Stacey's problem was solved when she found a domestic supplier, American Apparel, that could provide her with quantities of items in a wide range of sizes and colors.

But as a company grows, so do the options. Once Stacey's company had grown to a point where she needed to manufacture 40,000 thongs at one time, she began to look overseas and decided it made more sense for her to go with a Chinese manufacturer that could produce the goods for half the price.

The first time Stacey attempted to work with a Chinese factory, the language barrier was a big obstacle. So she contacted a broker/agent who could communicate what needed to be done. There was a lot of back and forth. Every detail needed to be approved—the weight of cotton, the colors/lap dips, style/cut, elastic waistband stretchy enough for a range of women's hip size, inside labels soft, outside labels clean white with the strong, bold red Blume label. The first shipment of a few thousand arrived, and Stacey was dismayed to find that the small/medium thongs, designed to fit women sizes zero to six, didn't stretch. Thousands of thongs had to be returned.

It was back to the drawing board, and Stacey tried yet another agent. This time, everything seemed to be going well. After a lengthy approval process, tens of thousands of thongs arrived at the Blume headquarters warehouse.

Stacey remembers that day very well, because it was like a scene out of a nightmare Christmas. As she opened box after box, it was clear that the thongs were all wrong. They were too thin and flimsy, and worst of all, they were teeny-tiny small. "The size small/medium was more like a negative zero," she told us on the show. "Nothing like the original sample approved. It was like the case of the incredible shrinking thong."

Big Idea Lesson: Stacey learned that the lure of a cheaper way is seductive, but it's never a good idea to put cost above quality. In fact, it can end up costing more.

Although the savings of manufacturing overseas would have been significant, Stacey recognized that the discount might come at the price of the Blume brand. So she bit the bullet and returned to American Apparel, where she was guaranteed the product she wanted. Her disappointment forced her to go back to basics.

RAMON RAY'S TECHNOLOGY RULES TO GROW BY

The Big Idea tech expert, Ramon Ray, is always a step ahead of the pack. He understands that technology is the key to

(continued)

growth. Without it, the modern business is like a jet with no fuel. So, listen up.

1. Spend money on technology as an investment—not as a cost. You spend money on insurance—right? You have a lawyer (most likely) and an accountant (for sure)—right? However, when it comes to spending money on technology, many of you ONLY spend money if you have to. You don't spend money on technology that you think you don't need. This is a mistake. If you are building a business to last, you must think of your technology spending as an investment. Don't think of where your business is now, but where it will be in five years, and invest in technology accordingly.

2. Expand your interactive options. You've heard all about Facebook, MySpace, LinkedIn, and a few dozen other social media tools that can help you connect with others. Many Web sites also enable you to comment, upload your own videos, and share your own insight with others. This is what web 2.0 is about. It's comparable to having a conversation with customers and letting customers have a conversation with each other about you and your product or service. You must have a great Web site, with awesome navigation and content. You must have an e-mail newsletter to reach people right in their e-mail in-boxes. You really should have a blog to foster more conversation and boost your Web site's rankings in search engines.

3. Go mobile. If you and your staff are sitting at desks all day long, I guess you don't need mobile technology. However, if you and your staff are traveling around (as I suspect most are) then you need to implement mobile technology solutions. This means that you can access your office wherever you are—e-mail, faxes, files. There's no excuse for telling a customer that they have to wait until you get back to your office. There's no excuse for telling a partner that you haven't received a fax someone sent you, or missed a voice mail because you were not in the office. Take your office with you.

4. Outsource your technology. There is NO need at all for you to manage and implement technology on your own. Sure, you are an expert in what you sell (be you a florist, computer vendor, lawyer, graphic artist, or media consultant). But you are not an expert in network security, data backup, or mobile technology. The only way you are going to maximize your use of technology is to outsource your use and implementation of it in your business.

Learn more by checking out Ray's site at www.smallbiztech nology.com.

The Hoopla Factor

Do you want to hit it big? Are you looking to super charge your business? Before you say yes, think about it carefully. A lot of people *say* they want to be big, but you've got to have what it takes. And what's that?

Gary Vaynerchuk has the model. Gary brings in fifty million dollars a year from his Web site, The Wine Library. When he started it in 1997, nobody was using the Internet to sell wine, and he had a great niche to fill. But Gary could have been complacent about it—nothing wrong with earning a couple million a year. Instead, he chose to be big, using a few simple principles, which he shared with us on *The Big Idea*.

✦ **The hoopla factor:** *Gary is a great spokesman for his site because he's full of energy and excitement. He makes it big by being a big, warm personality. Gary calls it the hoopla factor. "Be excited about what you're doing," he says. "Be as open and transparent as you can be. What makes you different is you. Let people get to know the person behind the product."*

✦ **Have a vision:** *Stay one step ahead of the pack. When Gary was starting, everyone was crazy about California wines. He was looking for the next trend, and it wasn't just what the forecasters were saying. "Reading trends is Death City USA," Gary says. "If you want to find the trends, get in the trenches." Gary has always read and answered every e-mail and talked to every customer. That's how he learned to look to Spain and Australia for the next big wine trend. Coming right up—Portugal and Greece.*

✦ **Put your chips on talent:** *As Gary grew his business, he invested in getting the best people. When he was just starting out, he paid himself less than his employees. Investing in people is social equity. Today he says, "I would rather have one million friends than ten million dollars."*

✦ **Spread your bets:** *Gary doesn't just hang with the wine crowd. "If you want to expand, don't just play in your own playground," he says. Gary is a wine guy who attends conventions in other industries, and talks to people in different types of businesses. It helps him stay fresh.*

Obviously, these principles work for Gary. You can't argue with a kid in his twenties who makes fifty million dollars a year.

DONNY'S DO: DON'T FORGET YOUR FIRST LOVE

We've all heard the story. A guy marries his college sweetheart, and she is the love of his life. She is completely devoted to him, and is willing to make every conceivable sacrifice to support his success. Hand in hand, they conquer the challenges of money, career, and family, and finally they've reached the peak. They're living in their dream house, raising fantastic kids, comfortable and content with what they've built. The hard-scrabble days are behind them. And then he leaves her. He walks out the door, saying he's going to follow a new love.

Don't let this happen to you. No, I'm not giving marriage advice. I am, however, offering advice of the heart. Once you get big, stay true to your first love—that original burning ember that propelled you to risk it all and do something unique and daring with your life. Don't walk out on yourself.

Conclusion:
This *Is* the Big Idea

A t *The Big Idea*, we write on the walls. No kidding. The walls of our brainstorm room—called the "Yes" room—are covered with a whiteboard surface that allows us to express ideas for the show with multicolored erasable markers. Those walls are always packed with scribbles, lists, titles, and concepts in the making. Some of the show's best segments, like "Keeping the Dream Alive," "Success Intervention," and "Million Dollar Idea," made their first appearance on the walls of our "Yes" room.

I'm the front man for *The Big Idea*, but the heart of the show is found in the team of incredible people who put it together. These are pros, many of whom have worked in television for years—long before my humble entrance on the scene. What awes me every day is how fired up they are. They take our mission to heart. *The Big Idea* IS their big idea. And they live it. On their off hours, they're out wandering the grocery aisles, camping out at the malls, walking around with their antennae out. You'd be surprised to hear how many of our guests were discovered through the ordinary lives of the people who put the show together.

And that's the way it should be. We're preaching creativity, innovation, and awareness. We're in the business of promoting ideas, so we try to breathe in that aura of possibility. *The Big Idea* has been life changing for all of us.

And our viewers? Each show brings in hundreds of e-mails, and the most common statement we get is the promise "I *will* be on your show." They're putting a stake in the ground, claiming a piece of the dream that they know is available to them. I fully expect to see many of them one day, sitting in the chair across from me, basking in the spotlight. The moms and geeks and comedians and cooks and technicians and builders and tailors and artists and brainiacs—everyone's welcome.

Is this a great country or what?

Appendix A

Are you ready to get started? Here are twelve steps and fifty questions to put you on your way to the American dream. No matter what your business, it's essential to ask the right questions. Use these as an active blueprint, filling in the answers from the advice and resources in this book, your independent research, and your gut.

STEP 1: WRITE YOUR MISSION STATEMENT

1. Who are you? Your future customers will want to know. The way you describe yourself will be the basis for the human story behind everything you do.
2. What do you want in life and business? Where do you want to be in two years . . . five years . . . ten years?
3. What is your motivation for starting your own business?
4. Do you have a level of passion for your idea that can't be dampened? How have you demonstrated that passion so far?

STEP 2: DESCRIBE YOUR PRODUCT OR SERVICE IDEA

5. What is your idea? Be as clear and succinct as possible. Imagine you are describing it to a potential customer.
6. What is unique about your idea? What problem does it solve? What is the benefit your product/service will provide?
7. Is your idea a new product/service, or an enhancement to an existing product/service?
8. If it's a product, have you made a drawing or diagram—or can you find someone who will?

STEP 3: CONDUCT MARKET RESEARCH

9. What category is your business idea? What is the current sales climate in your category?
10. Is there a product or service currently out there that is similar to yours?
11. Have you researched the price, packaging, and selling methods of similar products? Have you tried those products and made a distinction between them and yours?
12. What is the market for your product/service? Who are your potential customers? How old are they, where do they live, what other kinds of products do they buy?
13. Have you read everything you can get your hands on about starting a business, selling a product, and keeping your sanity?

STEP 4: CREATE YOUR BUSINESS PLAN

14. How would you describe your business operational concept? This goes beyond the description of your product/service to how you actually plan to conduct business. Will you have a physical store or office, a virtual store, a home office, etc.? Where do you envision your product/service being sold?
15. How will your business be staffed?

16. Have you created a business budget? What is your operating financial statement—including projected income and outlay?
17. How will your business be funded?
18. What are the lending sources that fund businesses like yours?
19. What is your funding pitch to possible investors? Memorize it!
20. Are you willing to trade equity for investment, and if so, how much?

STEP 5: BUILD YOUR NETWORK

21. Have you approached people in your field or those you admire to be your mentors? Remember, you don't have to know these people. You might be surprised to find others happy to help you if you are passionate about your idea. Have you reached out to people who have inspired you?
22. Are there business associations in your community, such as the chamber of commerce, women's association, or other group you can join?
23. Are there seminars, classes, or other learning opportunities that can also serve as networking opportunities?
24. Are there local charities that attract business peers?
25. Does your field have a trade magazine, trade show, annual event, or community?
26. Have you made an effort to keep in touch with former classmates, colleagues, friends, and neighbors?

STEP 6: FORMALIZE YOUR IDEA

27. Have you consulted a lawyer to help you protect your business interests?
28. Have you consulted a financial planner?
29. What is the ownership of your company?

30. What is the logo/name you will trademark?
31. Have you applied for trademark, copyright, and/or patent protection?

STEP 7: CREATE A PROTOTYPE

32. Do you have salesworthy working samples of your product?
33. Have you researched potential sources for prototype development?

STEP 8: HOLD FOCUS GROUPS

34. Have you tested your idea on friends and family? (Be sure to keep a record of their responses.)
35. Have you tested your product or service in free/friendly environments (street fairs, church socials, yard sales, etc.)? Have you given it away for nothing in exchange for feedback?
36. Have you asked local retailers for their opinions about your product or service?

STEP 9: FIND A MANUFACTURER AND DISTRIBUTOR

37. Have you conducted a search for manufacturers in your industry?
38. Have you noted the manufacturers of quality products that are similar?
39. Have you received estimates from a variety of manufacturers?

STEP 10: LAUNCH YOUR WEB SITE

40. Will you be selling your product/service online, or just advertising it there?
41. Do you have a Web developer to create your site?
42. Have you selected and registered a domain name that is consistent (the same) with your company name?

STEP 11: PUBLICIZE YOUR IDEA

43. Have you compiled a media kit?

44. What are the key points you want to make in your press release?

45. What are the editorial outlets that might be interested in your story?

STEP 12: PITCH POTENTIAL SUPPLIERS/CUSTOMERS

46. What's your pitch script? Have you memorized it?

47. Have you pitched your product/service in your local area?

48. Have you made a list of every potential buyer and started making the calls?

49. Have you submitted your product to QVC for consideration?

50. Have you reserved a booth at the next trade show in your industry?

Appendix B

THE BIG IDEA TOOLBOX
A RESOURCE GUIDE FROM MIND TO MARKET

The Big Idea Experts

- Lucky Napkin (www.luckynapkin.com): Amilya Antonetti and her team of experts help people launch their business ideas.
- Edge Consulting (www.drdoug.com): Dr. Doug Hirschhorn, a leading performance coach, shows you how to get the job done.
- Obsidian Launch (www.obsidianlaunch.com): Michael Michalowicz partners with first-time entrepreneurs who are willing to give their all.
- Smallbiztechnology (www.smallbiztechnology.com): Ramon Ray shows how to use technology to grow a business.

General Guidance for Entrepreneurs

- Startupnation.com (www.startupnation.com): Real-world business advice for new entrepreneurs.

✦ Jen Groover Productions (www.jengroover.com): Support for innovators with big ideas.

✦ OneCoach (www.onecoach.com): Business coaching for small businesses and start-ups.

✦ *Entrepreneur* magazine (www.entrepreneur.com): The leading publication for small businesses.

✦ *Millionaire Blueprints* magazine (www.millionaireblueprints .com): Self-made millionaires show how it's done.

✦ Unstoppable Enterprises, Inc. (www.unstoppable.net): Inspiring people to reach their dreams.

Resources for Women Entrepreneurs

✦ *PINK* magazine (www.pinkmagazine.com): The magazine for women in business.

✦ Women Entrepreneurs, Inc. (www.we-inc.org): A coaching, networking, and advocacy source for women entrepreneurs.

✦ *Mom's Business Magazine* (www.momsbusinessmagazine .com): A guide for home businesses.

✦ Moms in Business Network (www.mibn.org): A national network dedicated to supporting working mothers and their businesses.

Resources for Social Entrepreneurs

✦ The Institute for Social Entrepreneurs (www.socialent.org): Provides seminars, workshops, and consulting services for social entrepreneurs in the United States and around the world.

✦ Commongood Careers (www.commongoodcareers.org): A nonprofit job search firm that is dedicated to helping today's most effective social entrepreneurs hire the best talent.

✦ Idealist.org (www.idealist.org): A global clearinghouse of nonprofit and volunteer resources.

✦ Citizens for Global Solutions (www.globalsolutions.org): A grassroots organization that inspires Americans to get involved in the world.

Resources for Second Life Success

+ The Service Corps of Retired Executives—SCORE (www .score.org): A resource partner of the Small Business Administration (SBA) dedicated to entrepreneur education and the formation, growth, and success of small businesses nationwide.
+ AARP (www.aarp.org): The organization for Americans over fifty.
+ RetirementJobs.com (www.retirementjobs.com): Matches companies friendly to over-fifty workers with job seekers.
+ Workforce 50 (www.workforce50.com): An employment resource for older Americans.
+ Retired Brains (www.retiredbrains.com): Connects older workers with employment and nonprofit opportunities.

Resources for Inventors

+ U.S. Patent and Trademark Office (www.uspto.gov): The first stop for patent, trademark, and copyright information.
+ Mom Inventors (www.mominventors.com): Tools and resources for inventing moms.
+ *Inventors Digest*—"The Magazine for Idea People" (www .inventorsdigest.com).
+ The Inventors Assistance Center (1-800-786-9199): Basic information on filling out patent applications.
+ INPEX (www.inpex.com): The largest trade show for inventors.
+ Enventys (www.enventys.com): Integrated solutions for product development.
+ Everyday Edisons (www.everydayedisons.com): A PBS television show that introduces viewers to the process of

invention and helps them understand how to take their own ideas to the next level.

+ IdeaTango (www.ideatango.com): A resource Web site for inventors and businesses.

+ QVC (www.qvcproductsearch.com): Find out how you can present your idea to QVC or participate in one of its product search events.

Resources for Green Businesses

+ GreenBiz.com (www.greenbiz.com): News on green businesses and sustainable business practices.

+ GreenDreams (www.greendreams.com): A guide to green business practices.

+ Greenopia (www.greenopia.com): A guide to doing everything you do—greener.

Manufacturing Marketplace

+ Global Manufacturing Marketplace (www.mfgquote.com): Find suppliers and get quotes online.

+ ThomasNet (www.thomasnet.com): A comprehensive source for suppliers.

+ Manufacturing.gov (www.manufacturing.gov): A one-stop manufacturing resource from the federal government.

+ Alibaba (www.alibaba.com): An independent Web site that helps you connect with international manufacturers.

Web Domain Names

+ GoDaddy.com (www.godaddy.com): The world's largest domain name registrar.

+ Network Solutions (www.networksolutions.com): Domain names and registration information.

+ Register.com (www.register.com): Domain registration site.

Packaging Resources
+ *Package Design Magazine* (www.packagedesignmag.com):
  News and information for professional package designers.
+ TheDieline.com (thedieline.com): The leading package
  design blog.

Publicity
+ The Public Relations Society of America (www.prsa.org):
  Largest professional association of public relations profes-
  sionals.
+ PRWeb.com (www.prweb.com): A press release writing and
  distribution service on the Web.
+ The Publicity Hound (www.publicityhound.com): A how-to
  site for publicizing your business.
+ Publicity Insider (www.publicityinsider.com): A publication
  for PR-hungry businesses.
+ *Brandweek* (www.brandweek.com): The source for brand-
  ing news and advice.

Networking
+ LinkedIn.com (www.linkedin.com): An online network of
  more than 20 million experienced professionals from
  around the world, representing 150 industries.
+ Zoom Information Inc. (www.zoominfo.com): An extensive
  business search engine with profiles on more than thirty-five
  million people and three million companies.
+ BUZGate—Business Utility Zone Gateway (www.buzgate
  .org): A resource portal for start-ups and small businesses.

Business Funding

FINANCIAL COACHING
+ The Money Coach (www.themoneycoach.com): A
  step-by-step guide to growing your wealth.

✦ Money and Happiness.com (www.moneyandhappiness
.com): Laura Rowley's business and finance advice—with
the right attitude.

PEER-TO-PEER LENDING

✦ LendingClub.com (www.lendingclub.com): A personal loan
and lending investment company.
✦ Prosper.com (www.prosper.com): Personal peer lending, up
to $2,500.
✦ Zopa.com (www.zopa.com): A site for lenders and borrowers.

LOANS

✦ Small Business Administration (www.sba.gov): The government's full-service department for helping small businesses,
including a variety of special loan programs.
✦ Count Me In (www.countmein.org): Resources for women
entrepreneurs.

ANGEL INVESTORS

✦ The Angel Capital Education Foundation (www.angel
capitaleducation.org): A charitable organization for research
and information in the field of angel investing.
✦ The Angel Capital Association (www.angelcapital
association.org): A professional alliance of angel groups.

VENTURE CAPITAL

✦ Topspin Partners (www.topspinpartners.com): A venture
capital firm.
✦ National Venture Capital Association (www.nvca.org): An
information and support tool for businesses seeking venture
capital.
✦ Springboard Enterprises (www.springboardenterprises.org):

A national nonprofit organization that accelerates women's access to equity markets.

Staffing

+ Elance.com (www.elance.com): Freelance programmers, graphic designers, copywriters, and consultants bid on your projects.
+ Guru.com (www.guru.com): A global network of freelance professionals.
+ GetFriday.com (www.getfriday.com): A source for virtual office assistants.

Trade Shows

+ Trade Show Exhibitors Association (www.tsea.org): Provides a comprehensive array of trade show resources and information to sales, marketing, and management professionals who use trade shows and events to promote their products and services.
+ International Association of Exhibitions and Events (www.iaee.com): Represents the interests of more than 3,500 trade show and exposition managers globally.
+ Corporate Event Marketing Association (www.cemaonline.com): A nonprofit organization dedicated to serving event and marketing professionals in all sectors of the technology industry by providing educational and networking opportunities.
+ Comprehensive Trade Show Vendor Resource (www.trade-show-vendors.com): Online trade show guide offering hundreds of hand-picked trade show resources for successful events, business meetings, and conferences. The guide includes sources for event promotion, booth attractions, convention planning services, giveaways, booth design, lodging, transportation, and more.

✦ The Trade Show News Network (www.tsnn.com): Publications devoted to trade show news and ideas.

✦ *Tradeshow Week* (www.tradeshowweek.com): The magazine of the trade show industry.

✦ *The Roadmap to Success: The Ultimate Toolkit for Entrepreneurs and Business Owners: The Big Idea's "Road to CES"* on CD (order at www.cnbc.com).

Entrepreneur's Bookshelf

✦ *Employee to Entrepreneur: The Employee's Guide to Entrepreneurial Success,* by Suzanne Mulvehill.

✦ *The Mom Inventors Handbook: How to Turn Your Great Idea into the Next Big Thing,* by Tamara Monosoff.

✦ *Mommy Millionaire: How I Turned My Kitchen Table Idea into a Million Dollars and How You Can, Too,* by Kim Lavine.

✦ *Earn What You're Worth,* by Nicole Williams.

✦ *Zero to One Million: How I Built a Company to $1 Million in Sales,* by Ryan Allis.

✦ *A Million Bucks by 30: How to Overcome a Crap Job, Stingy Parents, and a Useless Degree to Become a Millionaire Before (or After) Turning Thirty,* by Alan Corey.

✦ *The Toilet Paper Entrepreneur,* by Mike Michalowicz.

✦ *Make More, Worry Less,* by Wes Moss.

✦ *Negotiation Genius,* by Deepak Malhotra and Max H. Bazerman.

✦ *Bounce!: Failure, Resilience, and Confidence to Achieve Your Next Great Success,* by Barry J. Moltz.

✦ *The Age of Miracles: Embracing the New Midlife,* by Marianne Williamson.

✦ *How Starbucks Saved My Life: A Son of Privilege Learns to Live Like Everyone Else,* by Michael Gates Gill.

✦ *Young Bucks: How to Raise a Future Millionaire,* by Troy Dunn.

+ *Money and Happiness: A Guide to Living the Good Life*, by Laura Rowley.
+ *Free Publicity: A TV Reporter Shares the Secrets for Getting Covered on the News*, by Jeff Crilley.
+ *Under the Radar: Talking to Today's Cynical Consumer*, by Jonathan Bond and Richard Kirshenbaum.
+ *Prepare to be a Millionaire*, by Tom Spinks, Kimberly Spinks Burleson, and Lindsay Spinks Shepherd.
+ *The Education of an Accidental CEO: Lessons Learned from the Trailer Park to the Corner Office*, by David Novak.
+ *How to Change the World: Social Entrepreneurs and the Power of New Ideas*, by David Bornstein.
+ *The Virtual Handshake: Opening Doors and Closing Deals Online*, by David Teten and Scott Allen.
+ *Often Wrong, Never in Doubt: Unleash the Business Rebel Within*, by Donny Deutsch with Peter Knobler.

Appendix C

THE BIG IDEA COMMUNITY

The Big Idea is more than a television show, and more than a book. It's a community. Follow the links to the entrepreneurs and experts we've featured, and join their millionaire community.

CALLING ALL DREAMERS
   Nathan Sawaya—www.brickartist.com
   Taryn Rose—www.tarynrose.com

NO EXPERIENCE NECESSARY
   Fizzy Lizzy (Lizzy Morrill)—www.fizzylizzy.com
   The Laundress (Lindsey Wieber and Gwen Whiting)—www
      .thelaundress.com
   The Wing Zone (Matt Friedman and Adam Scott)—www
      .wingzone.com
   The Glen Meakem Program—www.glenmeakem.com
   Soapworks (Amilya Antonetti)—www.amilya.com

WHY MAKE SOMEONE ELSE RICH?

Butler Bag (Jen Groover)—www.butlerbag.com

The Great American Pretzel Company (John Ruf)—
www.greatamericanpretzel.com

Terra Chips (Dana Sinkler and Alex Dzieduszychi)—
www.terrachips.com

Ramy Cosmetics (Ramy Gafni)—www.ramy.com

MAKE LOVE NOT WORK

Jeff Foxworthy—www.jefffoxworthy.com

Pearls Before Swine (Stephan Pastis)—www.comics.com/
comics/pearls

The Mydols (Judy Davids)—www.mydols.com

SalonTea (Tracy Stern)—www.salontea.com

Rick's Picks (Rick Field)—www.rickspicksnyc.com

THERE'S GOTTA BE A BETTER WAY

Spanx (Sara Blakely)—www.spanx.com

QuickSeals (Denise Bein)—www.quickseals.com

Just a Drop (Luc Galbert)—www.justadrop.net

iHearSafe Earbuds (Christine Ingemi)—www.ihearsafe.com

The French Twister (Lisa Lloyd)—www.lloydmarketinggroup
.com

Peanut Shell Baby Sling (Alicia Shaffer)—www.goo-ga.com

SCOTTeVEST (Scott Jordan)—www.scottevest.com

The Bagel Guillotine/Larien Products (Rick Ricard)—www.larien
.com

Strap Tamers (Noel Goldman)—www.straptamers.com

WHY DIDN'T I THINK OF THAT?

How's My Nanny? (Jill Starishevsky)—www.howsmynanny.com

QuiqLite (Brian Quittner)—www.quiqlite.com

Cereality (David Roth and Rick Bacher)—www.cereality.com

Vita Coco Coconut Water (Michael Kirban and Ira Liran)—www
.vitacoco.com

MadPackers (Brian Altomare)—www.madpackers.com

Monster Cable (Noel Lee)—www.monstercable.com

Flexflops (Stacey Kirsch)—www.flexflop.com

The Original Runner Company—www.originalrunners.com

SingleTease—www.singletease.com

KanDi Swim (Dani Kates)—www.kandiswim.com

BREAK OUT OF THE BOX

Ugly Talent NY (Simon Rogers)—www.uglyny.com

SENDaBALL (Melissa and Michele Sipolt)—www.sendaball.com

Bulldog Gin (Anshuman Vohra and David Kanbar)—www
.bulldoggin.com

The Shoshanna Collection (Shoshanna Lonstein
Gruss)—available at fine stores

CHANGE THE WORLD WITH A SIMPLE IDEA

Life is Good (John and Bert Jacobs)—www.lifeisgood.com

TOMS Shoes (Blake Mycoskie)—www.tomsshoes.com

WHY NOT ME?

Alton Brown, Food Network—www.altonbrown.com

Miley Cyrus, Hannah Montana—www.mileycyrus.com

Gary Coxe—www.garycoxe.com

TriBond (Tim Walsh, Dave Yearick, and Ed Muccini)—www
.tribond.com

CoolTronics (Tyler Dikman)—www.cooltronics.com

THE GUT CHECK MOMENT

Tarte Cosmetics (Maureen Kelly)—www.tartecosmetics.com

Sandra Lee, Food Network—www.semihomemade.com

Martha Stewart—www.marthastewart.com

Donald Trump—www.trump.com

Sean Combs, Diddy—www.diddy.com

Damzl (Heather Birdwell)—www.damzl.com

Subway (Fred DeLuca)—www.subway.com

THEY TOLD ME I'D NEVER MAKE IT

Tom Widgery (Jet Pack International)—www.jetpackinternational .com

PINK magazine (Cynthia Good)—www.pinkmagazine.com

Tennessee Bun Company (Cordia Harrington)—www.buncompany .com

SAVED BY A BIG IDEA

Rent-A-Husband (Kaile Warren)—www.rentahusband.com

Nadja Foods (Nadja Piatka)—www.nadjafoods.com

Dani Johnson—www.DaniJohnson.com

WHO SAID IT WAS TOO LATE?

Joy Behar—www.joybehar.com

Hot Picks (Stephen Key)—www.hotpicksusa.com

Marianne Williamson—www.marianne.com

Jesse Ventura—www.jesseventura.com

FROM ZERO TO MILLIONS

Paula Deen—www.pauladeen.com

Sinus Buster (Wayne Perry)—www.sinusbuster.com

Bear Naked Granola (Kelly Flatley and Brendan Synnott)—www .bearnakedgranola.com

Leslie Mayer—www.parentenergy.com

Cameron Johnson—www.cameronjohnson.com

OneCoach (John Assaraf)—www.johnassaraf.com

Laura Rowley—www.laurarowley.com

Unstoppable Enterprises, Inc. (Cynthia Kersey)—www .unstoppable.net

FUELED BY MOM POWER

Mom Inventors, Inc. (Tamara Monosoff)—www.mominventors
.com

FlipFOLD (Debbee Barker)—www.flipfold.com

Pump It Up (Brenda Dronkers)—www.pumpitupparty.com

Boogie Wipes (Mindee Doney and Julie Pickens)—www
.boogiewipes.com

Just Between Friends (Daven Tackett and Shannon
Wilburn)—jbfsale.com

Wuvit (Kim Lavine)—www.greendaisy.com

ALL IN THE FAMILY

Omaha Steaks (Todd Simon)—www.omahasteaks.com

Enterprise Rent-A-Car (Andy Taylor)—www.enterprise.com

Samuel Adams (Jim Koch)—www.samueladams.com

June Jacobs Spa Collection (June and Rochelle Jacobs)—www
.junejacobs.com

Amy's Kitchen (Rachel and Andy Berliner)—www.amyskitchen
.com

PEOPLE TO PEOPLE

Michele's Syrup (Michele Hoskins)—www.michelefoods.com

Desiree Gruber—www.fullpicture.com

Purdy Girl (Corinne and Nadine Purdy)—www.purdygirlnyc.com

Taser International (Tom and Rick Smith)—www.taser.com

Kirshenbaum Bond & Partners (Richard Kirshenbaum)—www.kb
.com

DOLLARS AND SENSE

Obsidian Launch (Michael Michalowicz)—www.obsidianlaunch
.com

JFL Innovative Investments (Jerry Lynch)—www.jflconsultinginc
.com

Alan Corey—www.alancorey.com

PERFECT PITCH

Blendtec (Tom Dickson)—www.blendtec.com

Ty Pennington—www.typenningtonstyle.com

Starbucks (Howard Schultz)—www.starbucks.com

Pacimals (Monica Williams)—www.pacimals.com

Zip-a-Ruffle (Kim Babjak)—www.kimcoaz.com

MAKE TRADE SHOW MAGIC

Lightglove (Bruce and M. G. Howard)—www.lightglove.com

Bug Labs (Pete Semmelhack)—www.buglabs.net

MoGo (Matt Westover)—www.newtonperipherals.com

H2O Audio (Kristian Rauhala)—www.h2oaudio.com

Sima Products (Ilana Diamond)—www.simaproducts.com

THE HUNGRY MILLIONAIRE

Container Store (Kip Tindell and Garrett Boone)—www
.containerstore.com

Yum! Brands (David Novak)—www.yum.com

Blume Girl Underwear (Stacey Blume)—www.blumegirl.com

Smallbiztechnology.com (Ramon Ray)—www.smallbiztechnology
.com

The Wine Library (Gary Vaynerchuck)—www.winelibrary.com

Index